SOCIAL SCIENCE & HISTORY DIVISION
EDUCATION & PHILOSOPHY SECTION

*Gifts and Ministries*

By the same author:

*Gifts and Graces*

# Gifts and Ministries

*by*

**ARNOLD BITTLINGER**

*introduction by*

KILIAN McDONNELL, O.S.B.

WILLIAM B. EERDMANS PUBLISHING COMPANY
Grand Rapids, Michigan

Copyright © 1973 by
William B. Eerdmans Publishing Company

All rights reserved

Library of Congress Catalog Card Number 72-96403

ISBN 0-8028-1497-2

Printed in the United States of America

Translated from the German by Clara K. Dyck

Chapters 1 and 6 were first published by the author in a booklet entitled *Treuhänder Gottes;* chapters 2 and 3 were first
published in *Charisma und Amt,* Stuttgart, Calwer Verlag;
chapters 4 and 5 were first published by the author in a booklet
entitled *Die Ordnung der Dienste.* Chapters 1, 4, 5, and 6 also
appeared in *Im Kraftfeld des Heiligen Geistes,* copyright 1968
by Oekumenischer Verlag, Marburg.

# Introduction

One of the major problems of the charismatic movement has been a lack of critical exegetical literature. There has been much use of Scripture and much popularizing with various appeals to Scripture, but little serious exegetical study. Charismatics in the historic churches have taken too uncritically the exegesis and theology of classical Pentecostalism. The historic churches owe an unpaid debt to classical Pentecostalism, a debt that has not even been properly acknowledged. Classical Pentecostalism has its areas of strength — evangelization, to mention only one — from which the historic churches might learn. But it would be a grave mistake to take over classical Pentecostal exegesis without careful reexamination.

The present book is a work for a broader audience by a researcher of the movement, who accepts the historical-critical method of exegesis, and who on that basis proceeds to examine the questions of "office" and charismatic functions in the church.

Though not myself a participant in the charismatic movement I have been a researcher of the movement for many years and I am well acquainted with its literature. In my judgment Arnold Bittlinger is perhaps the most competent theologian within the charismatic movement, and his writings will have large significance for Catholic as well as Protestant charismatics. He combines technical exegetical skills with the ability to recognize the strengths of movements both within the historic churches and outside. In the best sense of the word, he theologizes in the framework of a rich ecclesiastical and theological tradition. This makes it possible for him to act as a bridge-person between the charismatic movement and the established churches. Further, he can help the exegetically sophisticated, who are not greatly aided by much of the exegesis found in charismatic Pentecostal literature, to know that those who involve themselves in the charismatic movement are not under the necessity of embracing a hermeneutics that would be unacceptable at the professional level.

— KILIAN MCDONNELL, O.S.B.

# Contents

7

# I

## *Stewards of God*

As each has received a gift, employ it for one another,
as good stewards of God's varied grace: whoever speaks,
as one who utters oracles of God; whoever renders service,
as one who renders it by the strength which God supplies;
in order that in everything God may be glorified through
Jesus Christ. To him belong glory and dominion for ever
and ever. Amen (I Pet. 4:10-11).

The text cited deals with stewardship. Who is a steward?
If we consult a dictionary, we learn that a steward is a person who has been given the right of independent action, in
his own name, but to the advantage of another. In other
words, a steward is one to whom another has entrusted his
property for administration, in the expectation that he
will deal responsibly with it, that he will nurture and
multiply it.

When we confess our faith we acknowledge that God is
the Creator of this world. The world is his property. He is
the Lord of this world. But early in the Bible already we
read that God has entrusted the administration of the
world to a steward, namely, to *adām*, that is, to man. The
first chapter of the Bible depicts God as the sovereign ruler
of the world, who transfers the authority to rule to man in
the words, "Be fruitful and multiply, and fill the earth and
subdue it; and have dominion over the fish of the sea and
over the birds of the air and over every living thing that
moves upon the earth" (Gen. 1:28). In the next chapter
God is depicted as a gardener who entrusts the adminis-

tration of his garden to man, to faithful hands, in order that he might "till it and keep it" (Gen. 2:15).

These biblical statements form the basis of our entire civilization and culture. God's transferring to man of the commission to rule is God's Yes to technology — to dominion over matter; God's Yes to science — to mastery over thought and knowledge; God's Yes to poetry, music, and the plastic arts — to the mastery of word and tone, of form and contour; God's Yes to all of civilization and culture.

Since the commission to rule and preserve comes from God, it can only be carried out in dependence on God. This comes to expression in the early chapters of the Bible in the image of Paradise. To be in Paradise is to live in unclouded communion with God, to do what God does, to say what God says. Stewardship in the biblical sense, therefore, implies that God himself constructs and develops his creation through man. An example of this is found in Genesis 2:19, which records Adam's naming of the animals. "Whatever the man called every living creature, that was its name." The lordship of God over creation was practiced in a representative manner by the steward Adam, by man.

Man has not remained dependent on God, however. Rather, he has revoked his obedience in order "to be like God" himself, that is, independent of God. He did not wish to act and speak any longer as a subordinate of God, but to act and speak as was pleasing to himself. Where God is no longer recognized as the regulating center, order becomes disorder and cosmos becomes chaos. Moderation turns into excess, as expressed in the gruesome song of a descendant of Adam:

> *I have slain a man*
> *for wounding me,*

10

> *a young man*
> *for striking me.*
> *If Cain is avenged sevenfold,*
> *truly Lamech seventy-sevenfold*
> (Gen. 4:24).

The steward of God has become a rebel who wants to be like God and thereby loses his human nobility, which, Pascal says, consists of the fact that we need God.

The New Testament shows us another man as antitype to this first man who became a rebel — the second Adam, Jesus Christ. Jesus is the archetype and example for all stewardship. To him has been given dominion over God's creation. Paul writes that Jesus will reign as King until all his enemies have been put under his feet. "When all things are subjected to him, then the Son himself will also be subjected to him who put all things under him, that God may be everything to every one" (1 Cor. 15:28). That which has become chaos because of the rebellion of the first Adam will revert to cosmos due to the obedience of the second Adam. And how will that come about? In that God, the Creator, acts through Jesus and rebuilds and heals his destroyed and sick creation.

Jesus lived in such total dependence on God his Father that all his actions and words were God's actions and words. In John 5:19 he states, "Truly, truly, I say to you, the Son can do nothing of his own accord, but only what he sees the Father doing; for whatever he does, that the Son does likewise." In John 12:49f. Jesus says, "I have not spoken on my own authority; the Father who sent me has himself given me commandment what to say and what to speak. And I know that his commandment is eternal life. What I say, therefore, I say as the Father has bidden me." When Jesus spoke, his speech was God's speech; when he

11

served, he served in the power granted to him by God. Because God himself spoke and acted through Jesus, his followers judged that "he taught them as one who had authority" (Matt. 7:29) and that "he was a prophet mighty in deed and word" (Luke 24:19).

Just as the first Adam is the archetype of the rebel who misuses God's trust in him and spoils the treasure entrusted to him, so Jesus, the second Adam, is the archetype of the steward who administers that treasure judiciously and multiplies it.

Today mankind stands between these two images. By nature we are inclined to follow the example of the first Adam. We resemble the poor householder Jesus depicts in Luke 12:45, who misuses the authority given over to him and himself poses as lord. We want to be independent and control our own lives.

Thus a definite decision is required of one who wishes to follow Jesus, the second Adam. Man cannot live between these two fronts. Either he is at the disposal of God and lets God be active through him, or he is his own master and is thereby in the ranks of the adversary. There is no third possibility.

Whoever entrusts his life to the disposal of God will find that God installs him anew as a steward. He will experience God's taking possession of him through his Holy Spirit and working through him. He will discover that God himself speaks and acts through him. So, for example, Paul can write to the Thessalonians that he thanks God constantly for this — "that when you received the word of God which you heard from us, you accepted it not as the word of man but as what it really is, the word of God, which is at work in you believers" (I Thess. 2:13).

Acts 3:12 makes it clear that Peter was very conscious of God's acting through him in the healing of the lame man at the temple. That is why he energetically denounced the opinion of the throngs who believed that he had healed the cripple by his own "power or piety." A disciple of Jesus knows that he is unable to do *anything* without Jesus (John 15:5).

Paul, who calls himself an imitator of Christ (I Cor. 11:1) and asserted the same of other Christians as well (I Thess. 1:6), was so conscious of his close association with Jesus that he could say, "I have been crucified with Christ; it is no longer I that live, but Christ who lives in me" (Gal. 2:20).

What are the practical implications of this for us as Christians today? How can God be active through us?

God has given each of us certain aptitudes, capacities, and gifts that enable us to perform our service as stewards. With these we can help renew the creation, so that God's Kingdom may come to earth. These gifts are often buried in the natural man, and they are often misused and distorted in their application independent of God. But if we put our lives at the disposal of God, he will animate all the gifts and talents he has placed in us, and through them he will show his grace and Spirit in a new way. Our natural gifts thereby become gifts of grace.

Since we are not always so closely associated with God that he can work undisturbedly through us, we stand ever in danger of making ourselves independent of God's leading, speaking our own words, and acting in our own power. Thus, the writer of First Peter admonishes his readers to perform their service judiciously, as stewards of the treasure entrusted to them by God, so that they may constantly show anew God's *charis* (grace) in the *charisma* (gift of grace), that they may not speak their own words but permit God to speak through them, that they may not perform their service in their own power but in the power bestowed by God, "in order that in everything God may be glorified through Jesus Christ," to whom glory and dominion belong for ever and ever.

Having made these preliminary remarks, we shall now enter into a more detailed study of the meaning of *charisma* and of *ministry* and of the interrelationship between them.

# 2

## *The New Testament Concept of Charisma*

### 1. *The New Testament Evidence*

The concept of charisma is understood in the New Testament as "the concrete realization of divine grace." It characterizes a function — whether "ordinary" or "extraordinary" — that serves to build up the body of Christ.

The Old Testament uses the concept charisma only once, in Theodotion's Greek translation of Psalm 33:22. The Septuagint Greek translation has the word *eleos* — compassion or pity — in this verse. In Judaism the concept is also extremely rare. It is found twice in Philo, who elsewhere uses the word *charites*. For Philo both concepts characterize gifts in the realm of the natural. In the Hellenistic papyrus texts the word *charisma* is used four times to designate completely ordinary gifts. Like Philo, the Hellenistic writers used the concept *charites* more frequently.

In the New Testament the concept charisma is found most frequently in Paul's writings. Some twenty gifts are mentioned in connection with the word. The enumeration of the gifts in Romans 12 and I Corinthians 12 shows that they encompass a great breadth, from the administration of money to prophecy, from healing the sick to the state of celibacy. A systematic classification of the gifts is nowhere found in the New Testament.

Various attempts have been made to introduce an arrangement at least in these two lists of gifts. Most of these efforts reflect the ideas of the interpreter more strongly than those of Paul. The distinction made in earlier times between natural and supernatural gifts must today be viewed as outmoded in terms of both natural science and theology. I am personally inclined to distinguish four groups:

(*a*) *Gifts of proclamation* (prophecy, teaching, words of wisdom, words of knowledge, etc.).

(*b*) *Gifts of service* (administration of money, stewardship of possessions, chaplaincy, acts of mercy, deaconship, leadership roles, etc.).

(*c*) *Gifts of special power* (faith, healing of the sick, exorcism, deeds of power, etc.).

(*d*) *Gifts of prayer* (singing, praying in the spirit, interpreting, giving thanks, etc.).

All gifts serve (directly or indirectly) to build up the body of Christ. They are concrete manifestations of the love of Christ.

## 2. Misunderstandings

Two misunderstandings are to be rejected: (a) the suggestion that the Holy Spirit works through a man independently of his created state as a creature; and (b) the suggestion that every activity within the church is a charisma independently of the working of the Holy Spirit.

(*a*) *The enthusiastic misunderstanding.* The concept of charisma was already being reevaluated in post-apostolic times. The gifts have repeatedly been misunderstood as supernatural and miraculous phenomena. Where they emerged, they were wrapped in a mysterious veil and viewed as something sensational. Anyone who exhibited gifts like healing the sick, prophecy, or visions was, on the Catholic side, either revered as a saint or burned as a heretic. On the Protestant side such men were usually characterized as fanatics.

In all such cases the gifts of the spirit were understood as an enthusiastic or mystical phenomenon, as a more or less unnecessary addition to or embellishment of the "normal" Christian life. This narrowed conception of charisma did not take seriously the creatureliness of man. The human element was debased, and man came to be seen as only a lifeless instrument that serves God, sometimes without or even against its will. Man was no longer fully taken seriously as a man.

This conception is to be rejected from the perspective of the New Testament. Paul recognizes no distinction between natural and supernatural gifts. In his view the administration of money is just as much a charisma as is speaking in tongues and the work of *diakonia* just as much a charisma as the exorcism of demons.

(*b*) *The activistic misunderstanding.* The second misunderstanding is the understanding of the gifts as merely the normal activities and capabilities of man. On this view a charisma is exercised whenever a Christian does anything. In this way, for example, the nineteenth-century German theologian Eichhorn limited the gift of healing the sick to the "facility in healing that is acquired through the study of medicine." Even today one often hears the opinion that every man who in some way works within the church practices a charisma. Ushers, organists, preachers, leaders of youth programs — all are characterized as charismatics.

Here the concept of charisma is misunderstood to the extent that it is no longer asked to what end the individual person is gifted and commissioned by God. His more or less well-executed activity is characterized as a charisma. Yet it is by no means clear that a man who is working in a telephone counseling program automatically has been given the charisma of counseling. Indeed, experiences in the field of counseling show how fateful it can be for a man to engage in an activity without being gifted by God for that purpose. Mere activism within the church is not the same thing as charismatic deeds of the church. Whereas the creatureliness of man is not taken seriously in the enthusiastic misunderstanding of the gifts, the activistic misunderstanding fails to give the fall of man into a sinful state its due. Though Ernst Käsemann (appealing to I Cor. 12:7) characterizes the charisma as a concrete and individual realization of grace or of the Spirit, even grace and the Spirit are not so easily manifest concretely in fallen man. More often than not we encounter the "old Adam" as a very concrete individual. When Paul says in Romans 12:3 that no one should be active beyond the measure of his faith, he is presumably taking a position against such an activistic misunderstanding of the gifts.

The person who does not stand in "faith," that is, in a continually new dependence on God, is apt to consider many things as arising from his own talents or gifts that on closer inspection are nothing more than the imitation of a model that is especially impressive to him, or perhaps a pattern of behavior that is practiced in his immediate environment. His actual charisma may lie in a wholly other area, remaining buried as long as he continues to orient himself in the wrong position.

### 3. Charisma as a Function of the Body of Christ

If we ask ourselves, having rejected the enthusiastic and activistic misunderstandings, in what genuine charisma actually consists, we can perhaps formulate the following definition: a charism is a gratuitous manifestation of the Holy Spirit, working in and through, but going beyond, the believer's natural ability for the common good of the people of God.

God is the creator not only of mankind, but also of every single individual man. He has created every man as an original being and implanted definite and unexchangeable gifts in him. Through these gifts God himself wants to work in this world. When a man who is disengaged from God tries to lead his life according to his own opinions, his very being atrophies and he does not even exercise his actual function. Thus viewed from the side of nature we all act uncharismatically. Nevertheless, if a man opens himself to the work of the Holy Spirit, he becomes free to find his own originality and God makes use of the disposition that lies within the man in order to have his grace and his Spirit become visible for the salvation of the world. On the side of man this means continually new knowledge of his own inadequacy and a continually new awareness of his dependence on God.

The Holy Spirit does not work independently of the creaturely and evolving createdness of every man. If a certain person has a very narrow horizon, living and thinking for example only in the realm of piety, he will, if ever given the charisma of prophecy, deliver a correspondingly narrow prophecy, significant only for the realm of piety in which he lives. On the other hand, anyone who widens his horizon, who takes politics, economics, art, and the like into his sphere of interest, will also have a prophetic word to say in these spheres if the charisma of prophecy is granted to him. A committed and dedicated involvement within a definite realm or with a particular person is a presupposition for charisma to reach that realm or person.

For the charismatic (every reborn Christian is a charismatic!) there is no longer a boundary between this world and the world beyond. He views God and the world as realms that he can no longer separate from one another, not even in himself.

Anyone who exercises a charisma acts as a member of the body of Christ. Christ is today present in the world in the form of his church. He works today in no other way than through the members of his body. All members of the body of Christ are of equal value. But one can only speak of a charisma if the words or deeds are performed in dependence on Jesus (I Cor. 12:3), according to the measure of faith (Rom. 12:3), and as the realization of love (I Cor. 13).

# 3

## The New Testament Concept of Ministry

### 1. The New Testament Evidence

In designating the ministries of the church, the New Testament avoids concepts that have inherent in them an implication of power or dignity or the performance of a priestly function. As a rule the New Testament designates the function of the ecclesiastical official as *diakonia*.

The New Testament world is particularly familiar with two concepts of what we call "ministry" or "office" today. The first is *archē*, office in the sense of one who has supreme power and is the leader. This word is primarily a designation for a position of power. In the New Testament, for example, the Jewish and heathen authorities are designated in this way (Luke 12:11; Luke 20:20; Titus 3:1). Nowhere is this expression used in reference to the ministry within the church community. The second concept for office is *timē*. This designates a particular position of dignity. Christ's high priestly office of dignity mentioned in Hebrews 5:4 is expressed in these terms. However, the word *timē* is not used in the New Testament for a ministry in the Christian church. In the Greek translation of the Old Testament the particular designation of the priestly office is *leitourgia*. But (except for Rom. 15:16), this word, too, is not used in the New Testament to designate a ministry within the Christian church.

By applying the term *diakonia* to what we would today call "ministry," the New Testament chooses a concept that in no way designates a position of dignity or power.

An exact division of ministries in the New Testament is as difficult to make as a division of the charismata. All efforts at grouping will reflect the view of the interpreter to a certain extent. A division into "ministries for the local congregation" and "ministries for the whole church" seems to me the most appropriate one. Named under ministries for the local congregation (particularly in the pastoral letters) are: overseers (*episkopoi*), elders (*presbyteroi*) and servants (*diakonoi*). The ministries for the whole church are enumerated in Ephesians 4:11 — apostles, prophets, evangelists, shepherds, and teachers.

This division must not be construed as a static, unalterable pattern (especially not in the order of services). The New Testament thinks dynamically — even in its sequence of offices.

## 2. Misunderstandings

The following misunderstandings are to be rejected: (a) that the ministry does not require a supplementation by the charismata; and (b) that the charismata do not require a supplementation by the ministries.

(a) *Displacement of the charismata by the ministry.* The ministry gained an early precedence over the charismata. The opinion asserts itself (possibly already in the New Testament; see I Tim. 4:14) that appointment to a specific ministry entails a bestowal of corresponding charismata. Consequently, practice of the charismata is increasingly left to the minister. The general priesthood of believers, that is, the practice of the charismata by "nonofficial" church members, recedes more and more into the background.

Before Vatican II, in the Roman Catholic Church, a certain dignity (*timē*) was widely thought to attach to the ministry. Thus the Catholic manual of canon law by Eichmann and Mörsdorf states: "The position of leadership extends a preeminence to the clergy which is not afforded to the layman. . . . All believers owe a reverence to the clergy which is commensurate with the latter's rank and place of service." The minister also has a specific authority; thus the same manual states that "a prerequisite to the exercise of his power as shepherd is the existence of a relationship of submissiveness; the superior one is, after all, empowered to exert force over his subordinate ones. . . . The canonical minister is intrinsically entitled to a pastoral power." The concept of office held by the Roman Catholic Church was largely adhered to in the Protestant church as well.

(b) *Displacement of the ministry by the charismata.* The unbiblical concept of the ecclesiastical ministry as a position of dignity or power has been increasingly recognized in recent years and has come in for some severe criticism. The concept of the charismata is being discovered anew and reevaluated. In this process the difference between charisma and ministry is frequently suspended. The New Testament ministries are interpreted as "charismata."

Therefore the ministry is displaced by the charismata. Some believe, for example, that the New Testament prophet is only a Christian who has received the charisma of prophecy; that the evangelist is only one who has been entrusted with the charisma of evangelization; that a shepherd is a Christian with the charisma of counseling; that the teacher is one who has received the charisma of teaching. On this view, a special position is given to the office of the apostle. It is extensively understood to be a unique manifestation of the early Christian community. The apostle is regarded as a carrier of all the charismata. The ministries for the local congregation are also understood to be charismata. The bishop is regarded as equal in status with the shepherd and teacher. The elders are regarded as men with the charisma of leadership, and the deacons as people who are endowed with the charisma of *diakonia*.

The difference between charisma and office is extensively understood to be only a "difference in temporal claims." According to this interpretation particular ministries in the church are superfluous.

### 3. Ministry as Antitype of Christ the Head

What is a minister? A minister is a charismatic who has become conscious of his calling, according to his charisma, to a ministry due to the activity of the Holy Spirit, and whose calling has been recognized and confirmed by the church (cf. Gal. 1:15ff.; Acts 13:1ff.; Gal. 2:7ff.). All ministries are functions of Christ the head of his church.

How then can the New Testament ministry be rightly described? The charismata must not be pushed aside by the ministry, nor may the ministry be pushed aside by the charismata. Charisma and ministry belong together, just like the motor and the steering wheel in an automobile. A car with a motor and no steering wheel is dangerous. Church history has shown again and again that such uncontrolled charismata can create quite some havoc. It is easy to understand why the steering wheel has gained such great prominence. It is unfortunate, however, if, at the same time, the motor is increasingly devaluated. To be sure, it is essentially less dangerous for a car to have a steering wheel without a motor. One can steer in utmost peace without causing any kind of havoc — but at the same time the car does not move! Motor and steering wheel belong together. A motor without steering wheel is dangerous, but a steering wheel without motor is senseless.

In many respects the ministry has a steering function within the church. Its essence, however, is *diakonia,* service. And so it is in no way associated with a particular position of dignity or authority. The ministry has the responsibility of regulating the various charismata of the members, but not of hindering them. Thus, for example, Paul regulated the exercise of the charismata in his first letter to the Corinthians. But at the same time he was anxious not to dampen the spirit that was active in the charismatics (I Cor. 14:39f.; cf. I Thess. 5:19f.). The "official" prophets, according to I Corinthians 14:29f., have to keep silent when a prophetic revelation is bestowed upon an "ordinary" church member. The function of the ministry is to serve, to help in the development and regulation of the charismata. The minister too is a charismatic, but in him the charisma that characterizes his office is so pronounced and so predominant that he is assigned to a specific service within the church.

If the interplay between the charismata is presented in the analogy of the body of Christ in I Corinthians, the significance of the office becomes clear in the statements concerning the body and head in Ephesians and Colossians. The congregation is the body, Christ is the head (Eph. 1:22f.; Col. 1:18). What are the practical signs of Christ's position as head of the congregation? His love (Eph. 5:25), his sacrificing of himself for the church (Eph. 5:25), his concern for the purification of the church (Eph. 5:26). And how does the congregation respond to this activity of the head? It is subordinate to the head (Eph. 5:24). The New Testament ministry is an antitype of Christ the head. The minister legitimizes himself in that he loves the church, in that he sacrifices himself on behalf of the church, and in that he is deeply concerned about the spiritual welfare of the members of the church. His authority or power is purely spiritual in nature. He does not seek to have any particular outward prominence of dignity or power. The congregation reacts to the spiritual authority of its minister with obedience.

# 4

## Ministries for the Local Congregation

Let us now take a closer look at the ministries for the local congregation as they are discussed in the New Testament. It will be beneficial first to read from I Timothy 3:1-13:

> The saying is sure: If anyone aspires to the ministry of *bishop,* he desires a noble task. Now a bishop must be above reproach, the husband of one wife, temperate, sensible, dignified, hospitable, an apt teacher, no drunkard, not violent but gentle, not quarrelsome, and no lover of money. He must manage his own household well, keeping his children submissive and respectful in every way, for if a man does not know how to manage his own household, how can he care for God's church? He must not be a recent convert, or he may be puffed up with conceit and fall into the condemnation of the devil; moreover he must be well thought of by outsiders, or he may fall into reproach and the snare of the devil.
>
> *Deacons* likewise must be serious, not double-tongued, not addicted to much wine, not greedy for gain; they must hold the mystery of the faith with a clear conscience. And let them also be tested first; then if they prove themselves blameless let them serve as deacons. The *women* likewise must be serious, no slanderers, but temperate, faithful in all things. Let deacons be the husband of one wife, and let them manage their children and their households well; for those who serve well as deacons gain a good standing for themselves and also great confidence in the faith which is in Christ Jesus.

## 1. Bishops and Elders

(a) *What is a bishop?* Let us first try to determine the meaning of the word "bishop" (*episkopos*) as it was used during the time the New Testament was written.

In Hellenism the *episkopos* was, first of all, a political official. The Hellenistic kings sent overseers to visit the cities. In one text we read of King Attalus' sending an *episkopos* to Pergamum to examine the administration of the city. The *episkopos* was able to intervene; and if he found that the administration was not in order, he was able to reestablish the proper self-governing of the city.

In addition, the term *episkopos* was used in Hellenistic philosophical language. The Stoics spoke of an *episkopos tou kosmou,* an "overseer of the cosmos." This was applied to the philosopher, who was responsible for properly administering the cosmos, and ascertaining order in the world as a whole. The philosopher fulfils this task because of his recognition of the truth. He instructs the people regarding the ethical order of the cosmos. When the ethical order is upheld by the people, then the foundation of the world-order is assured.

Finally, we also encounter the concept of *episkopos* in Hellenism in various degenerated forms of meaning. It designates the supervisor, the accountant, the association treasurer. In Herodotus it also indicates the civil servant; and in Aristotle the herald who carries out a message.

The Jewish concept of bishop is closer to the New Testament concept than is the Hellenistic. All the settlements of the Essenes, a Jewish sect, were led by a bishop, the *mebaqqer*. The *Manual of Discipline* at Qumran stated: "The bishop stands at the peak of the many" (VI, 14). The expression "the many" refers in this context to the totality of such a settlement. In the so-called *Damascus Document,* which originated in Qumran, the activity of such a bishop is described as follows:

> This is the law concerning the overseer of the camp. He shall instruct the Many in the works of God and shall teach them His marvellous deeds and shall recount before them the happenings of former times. . . . And he shall have pity on them as a father of his children and shall carry them in all their despondency as a shepherd his flock. He shall unloose all the bonds which bind them that there may no more be any oppressed or broken among his congregation. And whoever joins his congregation, he shall examine him on his deeds and strength and power and possessions (XIII, 7-11, transl. by G. Vermes).

There are certain parallels between this Essene bishop and the New Testament *episkopos* of the Acts or the Pastoral letters. But it would be too much to conclude that the New Testament *episkopos* has developed from the *mebaqqer* of the Essenes. It is true that elements of the Judaic and Hellenistic milieu went into the New Testament ministry of the bishop, but the "episcopate" of the Christian church has developed on its own.

Along with the bishops in the New Testament we meet the elders. The passage we quoted at the beginning of the chapter does not mention these elders, but if we are to speak accurately of the ministries in the local congregation, we cannot ignore that of the elders.

In post-apostolic times the following order of rank differentiation can be observed: bishop — elder (presbyter) — deacon. Thus Ignatius writes to the Philadelphians (VII, 1): "Give heed to the bishop, and to the presbytery and deacons." This triple formula does not occur anywhere in the New Testament, where bishops, elders, and deacons are only mentioned separately or in the twofold group of "bishop and deacons." In the *Didache*, too, only bishops and deacons are mentioned.

The question arises, then, whether what Ignatius initiates and later develops fully is a false development or correct interpretation of the New Testament. Whereas many of the Protestant churches believe it is a false development, the so-called "episcopal" churches hold that the later development is organic and according to the will of God. They contend that everything is present in its germinal stage in the New Testament, but at that time it was impossible to differentiate exactly and to see distinct relationships. They believe that this germ cell later developed organically, according to its potential.

Let us look at some of the evidence that bears on this question. Titus 1:5 states: "This is why I left you in Crete, that you might . . . appoint *elders* in every town." Verse 6 goes on to state several prerequisites for an elder; and then in verse 7 Paul continues: "For a *bishop*, as God's steward, must be blameless." Are the words "bishop" and "elder" interchangeable in this text? Some interpreters think so, arguing that the word "elder" pertains to the person and "bishop" to his occupation. Others believe that a bishop was later chosen from among the number of elders, and that it was essential for that reason that the elders possess all the characteristics that would be required of a bishop.

According to Acts 20:17 Paul summoned *elders* from Ephesus to Miletus. When he addressed them, he said (vs. 28): "The Holy Spirit has made you *bishops*." The elders are omitted entirely in Philippians 1:1, and only the bishops (plural) and deacons are mentioned, just as in the passage from I Timothy we have cited earlier.

Chrysostom's answer to why the elders are not mentioned in Philippians 1:1 is that they "were formerly called bishops and deacons of Christ, and the bishops were called elders. That is why many bishops still write today: to the co-elder or to the co-deacon." Chrysostom is arguing from the style of the letters written by the bishops of those days. When a bishop wrote to a presbyter, the salutation was "Dear Co-presbyter"; when he wrote to a deacon it was "Dear Co-deacon." In other words, the bishop was reminding himself that these three ministries were originally combined in one, that of the presbyter.

I Timothy 5:17 speaks of a certain grouping within the ranks of the elders. Timothy is told to "let the elders who rule well be considered worthy of double honor, especially those who labor in preaching and teaching." Here is a differentiation between two — or perhaps three — functions within the ministry of the elder. It may have been possible that each of these functions was carried out by an "overseer."

I think we can make some progress here by taking a look at the cultural environment of the New Testament, and asking what the relationship was between bishops and elders in Hellenism and in Judaism.

In certain Greek towns (for example, Sparta and towns in the Doric colonies; it was different in Athens), a council of elders existed as the highest board of authority, the *gerousia*. (This word might be translated as "presbytery.") This board of elders elected (in part from the ranks of its members) "bishops" and "deacons" (servants) for the various tasks. A similar situation prevailed in the west, in Carthage and Rome, for example (though the Roman Senate naturally had much more power than the *gerousia* of a small Hellenistic town).

The Roman Senate ("board of elders") elected from its ranks both high Roman officials ("overseers") (for example, consuls and legates) and subordinate officials ("deacons") (for example, quaestors and tribunes). All

31

these officials had to report to the Roman Senate ("elders") regarding their activities. The Senate had full supervisory authority. After the time of Caesar, however, the office of the Emperor had developed within the Senate, and ultimately the Emperor placed himself above the Senate. One might ask whether a similar development took place in the church, that one single overseer elevated himself above the board of elders. Such an outcome need not necessarily be viewed negatively. Perhaps it was a historically essential development, as may have been the case in the Roman Empire.

What was the case in Judaism at the same time? Whereas the Greek *gerousia* and the Roman Senate supplemented their numbers from the old and noble families, the board of elders of a Jewish synagogue were elected by the congregation. This board of elders also called a "bishop" for each synagogue (the *archisynagogos*, whom we encounter oftentimes in the New Testament) and servants of the synagogue ("deacons").

Bishops and deacons were, therefore, elected by the board of elders both in the Hellenistic-Roman and in the Judaic domains, and they had special functions within the state or in regard to the congregation. Generally speaking, those elected were members of the board of elders.

Though we cannot be finally certain, it seems likely, on the basis of I Timothy 5:17 and parallels in contemporary history, that the *elders* were the ones who were actually responsible for the local Christian congregation. The names "bishop" and "deacon" were then designations for special functions within the council of elders, that is, within the congregation.[1]

[1] Alfred Adam concludes from I Clement 40-44 that the order of priesthood in the Old Testament is the basis for the office of the presbyter. He believes that the presbyters have divided themselves into bishops and deacons, commensurate with their activities. *Die Entstehung des Bischofamtes* (1957), p. 109.

32

(*b*) *How are the elders (or bishops) called?* According to Titus 1:5 the elders were to be installed by Titus, who had received an apostolic commission from Paul. The word used here specifically means to appoint, not to elect. Bishops, then, were not elected in the New Testament but appointed by the apostles or by those commissioned by them. The same applies to the elders. To be sure, the expression used for the installation recorded in Acts 14:23 means, according to its etymological derivation, "to choose by the raising of hands" (*cheirotonein*). By that time, however, the meaning of this term had already degenerated. Grammatical reasons make it impossible to speak of voting in this passage. The literal meaning is that Paul and Barnabas "voted" elders for each congregation. If anyone "voted" on the issue, it was only Paul and Barnabas, who conferred with each other and then cast a concluding vote! (Another possible reference of the Greek word *cheirotonein* here may be to the laying on of hands. In other words, the meaning may be that Paul and Barnabas installed the elders into their ministry by laying on of hands.)

In Acts 20:28 we read that the Holy Spirit has appointed the presbyters to the ministry of overseers. A passage in I Timothy is interesting in this respect. Chapter 4, verse 14 states: "Do not neglect the gift you have, which was given you by prophetic utterance when the elders laid their hands upon you." This passage seems to speak of a commission to service through the laying on of hands by the presbytery. An interesting analysis of this verse has been offered by Joachim Jeremias, who argues from Judaic parallels that this does not mean the laying on of hands *by* the elders, but *in order to "become"* an elder. The verse would then be interpreted: "Do not neglect to activate the gift of grace, which was given to you by prophetic utterance during the laying on of hands for your ministry as one of the elders."[2] Thus Timothy could have been directly appointed as elder, by Paul.

But, if an elder or bishop (overseer) was appointed by the Holy Spirit and by the apostle, how is the passage from I Timothy 3 to be understood: "If anyone aspires to the ministry of bishop, he desires a noble task"? How can one aspire to something that only the Holy Spirit, along with the apostle commissioned by him, can give? To answer this question we must examine the Greek word *orego* (translated here as "aspire") more closely. This word comes from the same root as the English words "stretch," "right," and "direction." A person who strives after something in the sense of *orego*, extends or "stretches" himself in the "right direction." (Whoever extends himself in the wrong direction destroys himself — see I Tim. 6:10.)

Plato uses this word in a very interesting way. He speaks of the soul as stretching towards its true being, towards its true essence (*Phaedrus* 65c). For every soul there is an ideal form in the invisible world, of which it is a replica and towards which it strives, in order to realize this ideal in the empirical realm. The soul constantly longs after its ideal form. It transforms itself into the image of this ideal by striving longingly towards the ideal (compare this with II Cor. 3:18). God himself placed this longing in man.

According to the apostle Paul, every person is an original as well. He has his very definite assignment in this world, which he is to realize. God has placed the longing after such a self-fulfilment into every person. When God has determined that a person is to become a bishop of a congregation, he awakens, simultaneously with the commission, a deep longing after this service in the person in

[2] J. Jeremias, "Zur Datierung der Pastoralbriefe," *Zeitschrift fur die neutestamentliche Wissenschaft* (1961), pp. 101ff.

question. This desire consists of a mixture of longing and fear. We fear the commission because it is always greater than that which we feel capable in ourselves. Nonetheless, this longing consists of an inability to do otherwise. If we do not wish to bypass God's commission to us, we have to act according to the innate laws of growth within us, just as a plant must realize a certain shape and color. Naturally, this kind of "striving" stands in direct contrast to all selfish, ambitious striving, in which the innate laws of man within us are not observed.

But man cannot, of course, realize his innate destiny forthwith, no matter how he strives to do so, unless other Spirit-led Christians also recognize and acknowledge this destiny and call him to a position commensurate with it. The same Holy Spirit who calls certain people to be bishops and instils in them a longing for this ministry clearly shows others — for example Paul, Barnabas, Timothy, and Titus — whom he has destined for this ministry.

So when Paul states that "if anyone aspires to the office of bishop, he desires a noble task," he uses a very strong term for the word "desires," one that expresses "greedy desire" and usually, in the New Testament, lust (Gal. 5:17; Matt. 5:28). In this passage, however, its object is a noble task. The man God commissions for a certain service suffers if he is unable to perform it. This is a frequent tragedy in today's churches: there are people commissioned by God for a certain ministry — whether apostle, prophet, bishop — who are unable to fulfil their commission, either due to their own disobedience or — what is much more common — because their fellow-Christians are too blind and egotistical to recognize and confirm the commission.

Why does Paul emphasize that one who aspires after the ministry of a bishop desires a "noble task"? One would think that the desire for a responsible commission is a very natural one. Apparently this was not so in the early Christian church. The Christians to whom Paul is writing obviously aspired more after the charismata, which were outwardly sensational, than after ministries related to a specific responsibility. This appears to be different today at least in the "official" churches. There are many who would like to become "presidents" or "bishops," but few long for the gift of healing, speaking in tongues, or of prophecy.

First-century Gnostics apparently looked on the ministry of a bishop with a certain disdain. The Gnostics claimed to live entirely in the metaphysical realm, speculating about angels and eternity while despising the earthly form of the church and wishing they had nothing to do with it. They preferred to be in heaven, in ecstasies and visions; they desired to speak and sing in new languages, along with the angels; they did not want to worry about everyday human trifles. They despised everything related to the material world — including the ministry of the bishop, who had to concern himself with the congregation on earth, with its administration, and so on.

So it is that Paul takes a stand to such an opinion and reevaluates the despised ministry of the bishop, calling it a "noble task."[3]

(c) *What constitutes the activity of an elder or bishop?* In Acts 11:30 and 21:18 we read of the elders as official representatives of the *local congregation* at Jerusalem. Acts

[3] The English word "work" is related to the Greek *ergon,* which is here translated "task." The ministry of the bishop is not one of meditation but one of work and productivity. It is an exhausting task. God-ordained activity is no mere busy activism. Organic growth (*ergon* is also the linguistic root of "organic") ensues where God works through man. Wherever a bishop called by God performs his task in dependence on God, organic growth will be present in the congregation. For an insight into the activity of an early Christian bishop, see F. van der Meer's *Augustine the Bishop* (1961).

14:23 tells of Paul and Barnabas appointing elders in the congregations of Asia Minor and entrusting them with the responsibility for these congregations. Similarly, in Acts 20:28, the elders in Ephesus are entrusted with the responsibility for the *congregation* in Ephesus.

This clarifies the difference between those who minister to the whole church and those who minister to the local congregation. The apostle has freedom of movement; the elder remains in one place. Elders need not give up their profession and devote themselves entirely to the work of the congregation; they are simply brothers who carry on in their regular occupations while bearing a special responsibility for the congregation.

What are the special responsibilities of an elder? I Timothy 5:17 mentions three — leadership, preaching, and teaching; James 5:14 lists prayer for the sick; I Peter 5:2 would seem to add the administration of finances and church discipline;[4] and Acts 20:28 adds the spiritual ministry. Comparing these functions with the lists of the charismata in I Corinthians 12:8-11, Romans 12:6-8, and I Peter 4:10-11, we see that an elder accepts those responsibilities that are in accord with his charisma.

At the same time, the person who has received the charisma of leadership is called an "overseer" or "bishop." Understandably, such an overseer has, with the growth of the congregation, also achieved a specific importance. Basically, however, the "overseer" is an elder, just like all the others. All the elders are "overseers" in a certain sense, each in that realm in which he is competent. One watches over the spiritual ministry, another over the teaching, still

[4] From the fact that an elder is not to be covetous or domineering, Bornkamm concludes that the administration of the congregational funds, as well as disciplinary power, had been entrusted to the elders. *Theological Dictionary of the New Testament,* VI, 665.

another over the money, and so forth. Everyone is an overseer in this sense, even though the title "overseer" (="bishop") has been applied only to the elder who is endowed with the gift of leadership.

Alfred Adam compares the bishop's task to that of temple priests (*mebaqqerim*):

> The activity of the *mebaqqerim* consisted of examining sacrificial animals for flaws and admitting the flawless ones. . . . In the church, where members brought the living sacrifice of obedience before God, these members were supposed to be "priests." The task of the *episkopē* included watching over the flawlessness of the members: examining baptismal candidates, admitting to the Lord's supper, combating false teachings, leading the Christians in their daily walk. . . . The ministry of the bishop comprises church discipline in its broadest sense.[5]

In summary, then, we can establish that the responsibility of the local congregation is in the hands of the elders; the elders are installed by the laying on of hands by the apostles (or their delegates); every elder performs a function that coincides with his charisma; the name "overseer" ("bishop") is gradually transferred entirely to that elder who has received the charisma of leadership.

(*d*) *The prerequisites for the ministry of a bishop.* Many of the characteristics that a bishop *must* exemplify are enumerated in verses 2-7 of the passage cited at the head of this chapter. (In the discussion that follows, we shall be substituting words occasionally in order to come as close as possible to the meaning of the Greek original.) The word translated *must* designates an unavoidable necessity, indicating that this passage describes the very archetype of a bishop. The bishop must, first of all, be *ir-*

[5] *Die Entstehung des Bischofamtes,* pp. 111ff.

*reproachable.* His private life must be free of anything that might cause offense. The next qualification is that he is to have *one* wife. What does this mean? Five interpretations have been advanced in church history. First is the opinion that the *one* wife is the church. Some Roman Catholic theologians conclude from this that a priest is not to marry at all, since he is already married to the church. A second point of view interprets it an opposite way: the bishop is to have *a wife.* That is, he must be married. This was manifestly the concept at the time of the Reformation. A third suggestion is that the guardian is to have *one* wife as opposed to many. The passage is thus seen as a prohibition of polygamy, which was permitted in Judaism and in Babylonian religion, whose teachers had two to three wives (a practice later adopted by the Moslems). It is possible that the Jewish Gnostics in particular were stressing the value of polygamy. A fourth interpretation considers this to be a prohibition of marrying again for those divorced. Finally, there are those who see it as a prohibition of marrying again after the death of one's own wife. This practice is maintained in the Orthodox Church up to the present day. The argument goes something like this: the bishop is the representative of Christ, the wife a symbol of the church. According to Ephesians 5 this symbolic significance can only then be maintained when the love of the "one" man is bestowed upon the "one" wife, just as the "one" Christ loves the "one" church.

Furthermore, it is required of the guardian that he be temperate. He is therefore not to be a person dominated by his emotions. He must be clear in his judgment and discreet in every direction. He is to conduct himself respectably, that is, he should adjust himself to the prevalent customs of dress, table etiquette, and the like. Above all, he is to be hospitable. Hospitality was taken to be part of the natural Christian duty in the ancient world, where there were few hotels and where the Christian missionaries traveled extensively. This is still widely practiced today in the East. The bishop must have an aptitude for teaching. The prerequisite for this is a constant readiness to accept the lessons being taught to him as well.

The further stipulation that a guardian not be a drunkard and not a ruffian gives a clear picture of the situation in the congregations of that time! (An old manuscript adds a note here, namely, that the bishop is not to be covetous.) On the contrary, friendliness is expected of him; he is to be open to everyone. He must be peaceable, which includes avoiding constant theological quarrels, and above all he is not to be a devotee of money.

Verses 4 and 5 require that the bishop lead an orderly family life. This is based on the presupposition that one who is not able to manage his own household will scarcely be appropriate for the position of overseer within a Christian congregation. His own children should be an example, in a certain respect, of the "obedience" and "dignity" required of every Christian. This verse makes it quite clear that all those things that are enumerated here cannot be required in a legalistic sense; rather, that this has to do with the archetype of a bishop, which this "earthly" bishop is to have before his eyes constantly, in order to "aspire" after it in the right manner.

The requirement of verse 6 that no new convert be called to guardianship, because he might then be tempted to fall into arrogance and slander, seems to be based on an experience of the early Christians, and it might well be observed today. Verse 7 again employs the strong Greek term for *he must* in stating the necessity that a guardian have a *good reputation* among non-Christians. A bishop who lacks such a reputation would be a burden for the congregation.

Does this description not depict an ideal figure, which can never be empirically realized? Certainly, no man will ascribe these attributes to himself. According to II Corinthians 3:18, however, the possibility exists that a Christian — and therefore also a bishop — may be transformed more and more, from one degree of glory into another, into the image of Christ. (This does not mean that we Christians will be without sin; on the contrary, the more we approach Christ, the brighter his light will shine on us and the more profoundly we will be aware of our sinful condition.) Church history gives abundant testimony to the fact that bishops such as have been delineated here were to be found again and again.

## 2. Deacons and Deaconesses

(a) *What is a deacon?* The word *diakonia* (=service) is used in the New Testament both as a designation for the charismata in general (I Cor. 12:5) and in reference to a special charisma (Rom. 12:7). Besides this, it can be found both in the designation of "ministries" in general (I Tim. 1:12; Eph. 4:12) and in the designation of a specific ministry, namely, the ministry of the deacon (Acts 6:1). Like all other ministers, the deacon is a charismatic. However, his charisma of *diakonia* is so pronounced as to induce the congregation to entrust him with a particular ministry.

What constitutes the ministry of a deacon? According to Acts 6, it originally entailed a distribution of provisions to needy members of the congregation, in "serving tables" (Acts 6:2). A kind of common life was prevalent, and anyone who had a surplus divided his property among the needy. It appears from Acts 2:45 that the donors originally distributed such gifts personally. No doubt this meant that some were served too generously while others were overlooked. Therefore an arrangement for a more equitable distribution had to be found. Thus we read in Acts 4:35 that the gifts were laid "at the feet of the apostles" (possibly the apostles sat on slightly elevated seats at that time). The donated gifts "were made to each according to his need." The use of the passive tense in this sentence may indicate that workers were, already at that time, entrusted with the distribution.

Then, in Acts 6, this ministry of the distribution of gifts is entrusted to men who are particularly adept at it, and this is accompanied by the laying on of hands. Thus the ministry of the deacon is concerned primarily with the welfare of others. In Judaism there had existed the so-called "daily pot," a feeding of the poor out of the provisions of the synagogue. In early Christendom, on the other hand, the poor were fed by voluntary gifts.

(b) *How is a deacon called?* The word "aspire" is not used in relation to the calling of deacons. Yet what we have said about the ministry of the bishop is relevant here too. God has placed such a strong charisma of *diakonia* in some people as to give them a "greedy desire" to realize this commission. I recently met a deacon who is performing an unglamorous service as caretaker of the aged. He was earlier employed as an artist, restoring sculptures in churches and in old castles. He told me that he had long felt a burning desire, while working at his earlier activity, to be concerned with living people instead of with dead sculpture. Although his present ministry, seen from the viewpoint of aesthetics, is the exact opposite of his former occupation, the present occupation gives him a far greater sense of satisfaction than the former did.

The deacon — like the bishop — is enabled to perform his service only if he has been commissioned by the congregation to do so. How such a commissioning came about can be read in Acts 6:1-6:

> Now in these days when the disciples were increasing in number, the Hellenists murmured against the Hebrews because their widows were neglected in the daily distribution. And the twelve summoned the body of the disciples and said, "It is not right that we should give up preaching the word of God to serve tables. Therefore, brethren, pick out from among you seven men of good repute, full of the Spirit and of wisdom, whom we may appoint to this duty. But we will devote ourselves to prayer and to the ministry of the word." And what they said pleased the whole multitude, and they chose Stephen, a man full of faith and of the Holy Spirit, and Philip, and Prochorus, and Nicanor, and Timon, and Parmenas, and Nicolaus, a proselyte of Antioch. These they set before the apostles, and they prayed and laid their hands upon them.

According to this report, the calling of the deacons comprises a threefold action. First, the apostles call the congregation together, explain the necessity of the ministry of a deacon and propose qualifications required of those to be chosen and concerning the division of tasks (vss. 2-3). Second, the congregation chooses seven men for this ministry (vs. 5). In contrast to the call of a bishop or elder, the congregation is here involved as well. Third, the execution of the decision of the congregation again reverts to the apostles, who pray for the newly chosen and lay their hands upon them. The laying on of hands demonstrates to those chosen that they are now duly empowered to fulfil their ministry. The laying on of hands is not an empty gesture, which might just as well be omitted; rather, it is an action which rightfully forms a part of the call of a servant.

Symbolic acts are very vital proceedings in the Bible, for

43

our body is included in God's act of salvation. Symbolic acts are not empty signs of picturesque actions. Rather, in the symbol, the sign and the object symbolized coincide. Where the sign is spoiled, there the object is spoiled also. (This applies especially to the sacraments; cf. I Cor. 11:27ff.).

(c) *The prerequisites for the ministry of the deacon.* The deacon must meet certain prerequisites, like the bishop, if he is to be a legitimate deacon. These are delineated in I Timothy 3:8-13. First of all, the deacon is to be respectable. No one must deem that he embezzles the gifts that have been entrusted to him. Two-facedness is particularly bad, since lying and cheating are closely related. If he were a drunkard or greedy person, he would similarly stand in danger of embezzling gifts. Thus, the vices a deacon must avoid are closely related to his commission. Since there is a danger for a Christian who works in a welfare role that he may do his service mechanically, it is required, furthermore, that the deacon be a Christian with heart and soul, that he "hold the mystery of the faith with a clear conscience." (The Christian faith is here compared to a mystery religion, which also expects a certain ethical purity from its adherents.) Verse 10, where a thorough examination of deacons is advocated, particularly shows that the danger of slander by outsiders was prominent in early Christendom. This is definitely not a reference to a theoretical examination, but rather it is meant to establish that this man has in his everyday life maintained reputable conduct consistent with the Christian way of life.

Verse 11 does not refer to the wives of deacons, but to female deacons, that is, deaconesses. We know from Romans 16:1f. that the early Christians had such female deacons. Apparently the particular hazards these women faced

were gossip, emotionalism, and untrustworthiness. Therefore it is required of the deaconesses that they speak no
slander, that they be sober and trustworthy in all matters.

After this digression concerning deaconesses Paul again
returns to the deacons in verse 12. They, too, are to have
one wife and to live an orderly family life.

But what is the meaning of the remarkable verse 13:
"Those who serve well as deacons gain 'a beautiful stage'
and also great confidence in the faith which is in Christ
Jesus"? In this verse Paul is confronting the false teachings
of the Gnostics. The Gnostics believed that the more
knowledge a man gains and the more he lives in visions
and ecstasies, so much the more he will release himself
from the material world that wants to hold him and he
will be carried stage after stage towards the heavenly
world of light. Thus, the Gnostic gains a "beautiful stage"
by means of knowledge and ecstasy. In contrast, Paul
says, "No, the beautiful stage is achieved by means of the
*diakonia.*" The Gnostics believed that, the more the body
was despised (either by means of asceticism or by enjoy-
ing life to the full), the more would he extricate himself
from material bondage and the more freedom and "frankness" the man would have. Paul, on the other hand, states:
"No, the more you remain rooted to this earth, the more
you are totally involved with service for this world, so
much the more frankness you will have and the more you
will live in the metaphysical reality as well." The more
clearly and distinctly the Christlike image is lived here on
earth, the closer is its relationship with the heavenly
prototype.

# 5

## *Ministries for the Whole Church*

Paul's words in Ephesians 4:11-16 will serve as basis for our thoughts on ministries for the whole church.

> And his gifts were that some should be apostles, some prophets, some evangelists, some pastors and teachers, for the equipment of the saints, for the work of ministry, for building up the body of Christ, until we all attain to the unity of the faith and of the knowledge of the Son of God, to mature manhood, to the measure of the stature of the fulness of Christ; so that we may no longer be children, tossed to and fro and carried about with every wind of doctrine, by the cunning of men, by their craftiness in deceitful wiles. Rather, speaking the truth in love, we are to grow up in every way into him who is the head, into Christ, from whom the whole body, joined and knit together by every joint with which it is supplied, when each part is working properly, makes bodily growth and upbuilds itself in love.

Paul here continues a trend of thought he began in the early part of this letter — growing up in every way into him who is the head. Verse 10 had spoken of Christ, "who also ascended far above all the heavens, that he might fill all things." In order to accomplish this task, Christ has instituted "ministries."

We shall ask four main questions in this chapter: What are the ministries referred to here, and what is their significance? What is the function of these ministries? What dangers threaten the growth of the body of Christ? How does healthy growth come about?

## 1. The Ministries for the Whole Church and Their Significance

In verse 11 we read: "And his [Christ's] gifts were that some should be apostles, some prophets, some evangelists, some pastors [shepherds] and teachers." The ministries in the church are gifts of Christ. Just as the charismata, the gifts of grace, are gifts of the Holy Spirit, so the ministries named here are gifts of the ascended Christ.

It is an old dispute whether Paul's enumeration of ministries in verse 11 mentions four or five different ministries. The church father Jerome felt that the last two are closely related: "He who is a shepherd must also be a teacher." On the other hand, the Catholic theologian Joseph Brosch argues for separating these two in spite of the fact that the article is missing in front of "teacher." He concludes that the two belong to one classification of persons, but not that the teacher and pastor are identical.[1] Eduard Schweizer takes an intermediate position on this question, suggesting that perhaps the ministries were originally separate but have come more and more to be linked in one person.[2]

These, then, are the choices for interpreting this passage. Some believe it refers to *one* ministry; others that it refers to *two;* and still others that one cannot know definitely. My own opinion is that this question is not of utmost significance. At any rate, we shall deal with the various ministries separately. It is left to the reader to decide whether or not he wishes to ascribe the two last-named ministries to one person.

Now let us look more closely at these four or five minis-

[1] Joseph Brosch, *Charismen und Aemter in der Urkirche* (1951), p. 117.
[2] E. Schweizer, *Gemeinde und Gemeindeordnung im Neuen Testament,* footnote 750.

tries. We shall deal in greatest detail with the ministry of the apostle, for there are several prevalent notions about that ministry which should be demythologized.

(a) *Apostle*. Both the name and the ministry of an apostle are frequently surrounded by such a halo that one is hesitant to apply the term at all to living people, instead speaking of apostles only after several centuries have elapsed and it is not recalled so accurately that these "apostles" were also only men. Thus it is well for us to put the concept "apostle" under the magnifying glass.

In the Septuagint Greek translation of the Old Testament we read in II Chronicles 17 of the reign of King Jehoshaphat. He sent out his princes to visit the various parts of the land. The same Greek expression is used here as is later used for the apostles in the New Testament; Jehoshaphat sent out (*apesteilen*) his princes with the commission to teach in Judah (vs. 7). These men not only made visitations, but they taught as well.

In later Judaism (through New Testament times) the "apostles" were ordained rabbis who traveled to the Jews living outside of Palestine — the *diaspora* — in order to gather money for the temple in Jerusalem and to supervise the congregations. Paul was probably one of these Jewish apostles before his conversion. We know from Acts 9:14f. that he traveled as emissary of the chief priests to Damascus in order to supervise and perform apostolic functions there.

It is an old Jewish maxim that "the apostle is the equivalent to him who has sent him," and in Judaism this is taken quite literally. This is not a matter of substitution; rather, the one who commissions is seen to be present in person. There is an interesting example of this in the New Testament story of the centurion of Capernaum (Matt. 8:5-13; Luke 7:1-10). It is not my intention here to force

48

these two accounts of Luke and Matthew into a harmonization, but I believe that this is a very typical example of how seriously an emissary, an "apostle," was taken. Luke reports that the centurion of Capernaum did not himself come to Jesus, but that he sent (*apesteilen*) elders and friends instead, and with them he sent the message: "I did not presume myself worthy to come to you" (Luke 7:7).

The Judeo-Christian Gospel of Matthew, on the other hand, reports without further ado that the centurion himself came to Jesus (Matt. 8:5). I believe that this is not a case of an inaccurate memory, but that here the Judaic understanding of the apostolate is taken seriously. When the centurion sends men to Jesus with a specific commission, he is himself present in these men. This reasoning may be difficult for us to follow, but this is the way the Jews actually reasoned. Again, when Paul is in Damascus under orders from the chief priests, this signifies that *in him* the chief priests are themselves present in Damascus. This indicates several nuances of meaning for the New Testament understanding of an apostle. We must once again understand a concept such as this in the way it was understood in the New Testament world, not as we generally understand it today after two thousand years of Western history.

In Hellenism the word *apostolos* means, first of all, "messenger," "emissary," of whatever commission it may be. In a special sense, *apostolos* is a technical term in the language of the sea. *Apostolos* refers to the fleet of ships or the expedition; and, in a transferred sense, also to the captain of the ship, "the admiral" who commands the fleet; and finally it is the "colony" founded by the admiral. Therefore, when a fleet left Athens and founded a colony somewhere on the shores of Asia Minor or of Sicily, all

49

these were "apostles" — the fleet, the admiral, and the new-found colony. All were legitimate representatives of their home town.

Thus the concept of the apostle has a very broad sense in Hellenism. All these interpretations are to an extent included in the New Testament concept of the word, at least in the imagination of those who read or heard of this concept at that time.

In the New Testament the identification between him who sends and him who is sent is emphasized primarily. Matthew 10:40, for example, records Jesus' saying that "he who receives you receives me." Again, in Luke 10:16 Jesus says, "he who hears you hears me." When an apostle speaks, Jesus speaks. The apostle speaks in the authority (*exousia*) of Jesus. John 13:16 stipulates that the "apostle" is to be treated like his master in every way: "A servant is not greater than his master" (cf. Matt. 10:24f.). An emissary of a small dwarfish state cannot take the same stance as an emissary of a world power; he cannot come forward with similar demands for the simple reason that he lacks a sufficient power to back him up.

The apostle represents his employer. People read the nature of Christ from the nature of the apostle. The Christians in Asia Minor and Greece never saw Jesus. They were only able to sense and know who Jesus is because they had seen a Paul. That is why Paul is able to make the bold statement: "Be imitators of me, as I am of Christ" (I Cor. 11:1). The Corinthians had no other way to imitate Jesus than to follow the example of the apostle Paul; abstract sayings about Jesus were much less impressive for them than this apostle in real flesh and blood.

After Pentecost the ministry of the apostle becomes that which lays the foundation of the church. Both I Corinthians 12:28 and Ephesians 4:11 speak in general terms of the apostles. Irenaeus listed the seventy whom Jesus sent out, according to Luke 10:1, among the apostles and specifically calls them by that name. In I Corinthians 15:5 and 7 Paul distinguishes between the circle of twelve and the rest of the apostles, apparently linking himself with the second group (vs. 8). Vincent Taylor has distinguished between four groups of apostles in the New Testament.[3] First there were the apostles in Jerusalem (the circle of twelve and James, the brother of the Lord). The conditions of their apostolic ministry are recorded in Acts 1:21f. Second, there were the apostles of Antioch (Paul, Barnabas, and Silas). Their commission consisted in the supervision of the Gentile churches. Apostles with local assignments among the Gentiles (for example, Andronicus and Junias, Rom. 16:7; cf. II Cor. 8:23 – "our brethren, they are apostles of the churches") formed the third group. Finally, there were those who performed apostolic ministries without being expressly called "apostle" in the New Testament. Timothy and Titus are representatives of this group.

Taylor designates the common characteristics of all apostles as follows: "They were aware of an inner call of Christ. This call was unmistakably attested to by the Holy Spirit and recognized and confirmed by the Church."

The New Testament offers us a particularly good insight into the apostolic ministry of Paul. Four characteristics of this can be clearly seen. The first is calling by God (Gal. 1:15ff.). Paul tells the Galatians that God himself has called him and that, after this, he has not conferred with flesh and blood anymore. The church father Origen believed that Jesus not only calls men to be apostles, but

[3] Vincent Taylor, *The Gospel According to St. Mark* (1959), pp. 626ff.

angels as well. In his commentary on the Gospel of John he writes:

> Jesus not only sends saints, but saints and angels. . . . For we shall not be amiss if we ascribe the name "apostle" to those also, of whom is written: "Are they not all ministering spirits sent forth to serve, for the sake of those who are to obtain salvation?" (Hebrews 1:14). . . . If one is an apostle because he is being sent . . . then the angels, too, are apostles of him who sends them (XXXII, 17).

A second characteristic of Paul's apostleship is setting apart by the congregation. Acts 13:1-3 speaks of this, and it is a part of the call of God. Five "prophets and teachers" in the congregation at Antioch are mentioned. Of these, Paul and Barnabas are set apart by the congregation, following prophetic instruction, and are sent into the world with a specific commission as apostles. However, such a commission is operative only for the time span and area for which they have been commissioned. Under some circumstances the commission may involve only a single congregation, or even, Origen argues, a single person, for whom the one sent, the "apostle," then becomes an emissary of God (*Commentary of John*, XXXII, 17).

The third characteristic is acknowledgment by the church as a whole. After Paul and Barnabas had been sent out by their congregation and had worked in Asia Minor, they strove to attain the recognition of the other apostles as well. Galatians 2:9 states that Peter extended the right hand of fellowship to Paul and Barnabas, which is to say that the apostolic ministry of these two men was acknowledged by the rest of the apostles also. Paul expresses himself very forcefully in this connection, indicating that he was anxious for this acknowledgment from his fellow-apostles, in order that his ministry might not be in vain (Gal.

2:2). He was concerned that the unity of the church not be disturbed under any condition, and he did not want the others to be able to say that what Paul did, did not concern them at all. If that were true, Paul felt, his entire ministry would have been in vain. We should pay close attention to this notion of Paul about division in the church, and realize how grave — indeed, how unthinkable — a division within the one church would have been for Paul.

The fourth characteristic is confirmation by the "signs of a true apostle" (II Cor. 12:12). In using this expression Paul appears to be picking up a phrase used by his Corinthian opponents, which he corrects and enlarges, but does not devaluate (cf. Acts 2:22; Rom. 15:19; Gal. 3:5; Heb. 2:4). It is noteworthy that Paul writes that the signs, miracles, and acts of power have been performed "in all patience." Certainly, Paul does not mean by this that they were achieved under particularly difficult circumstances; probably he wishes merely to stress that such miracles — quite apart from the fact that they are not unequivocal criteria (cf. Mark 13:22; II Thess. 2:9) — have a subordinate meaning as far as he is concerned. He actually feels like a "fool" (II Cor. 12:11) for letting his opponents in Corinth force him to enter into the issue of the miracles at all. Remember that, for Paul, the total apostolic ministry is achieved "in the Spirit." His weakness (II Cor. 11:16-33) is for him a more essential sign of the apostle than the miracles and acts of power that have been performed in him or through him (II Cor. 12:9-10). Ernst Käsemann writes: "His *diakonia* is no less a proof of the godly spirit for him than are the visions and revelations."[4] At the same time we must not forget Paul's stand before God, and his repeated experience of such "ecstatic" workings of power (II Cor.

[4] E. Käsemann, "Die Legitimität des Apostles," *Zeitschrift für die neutestamentliche Wissenschaft* (1942), p. 68.

14:18; II Cor. 12:2-4, 12). These experiences are, on the one hand, prerequisites for his total ministry (Acts 9:1ff.; Gal. 2:2; Acts 16:9f.; 18:9f.); they are not, on the other hand, for him essential miraculous phenomena. They are only essential to the extent that "reasonable" service arises from them (II Cor. 5:13; I Cor. 14:18, 19). Käsemann points out that

> the actual sign of the apostle is not seen in single incidents of power in action and in ecstatic experiences, but rather, in the continuity of an outstanding ministry in the congregation, performed sensibly and with charity, in patience and weakness.[5]

What, then, constitutes the task of an apostle? We read in a number of instances that the group of apostles made decisions. In the context of one of these (Acts 15:28), we read the famous remark "it has seemed good to the Holy Spirit and to us." Thus, the apostles make decisions that concern the congregation in the power of the Holy Spirit. I Corinthians 14:38 reveals that Paul had a certain authority relative to the congregations he had founded, for he states that if anyone does not recognize his own writing as a command of the Lord, that person is not recognized by Christ either. In I Corinthians 11 and following chapters Paul gives explicit instructions concerning the order of worship service, questions pertaining to communion, and the like. Jude 17 and Revelation 21:14 would indicate the apostles are representatives of normative preaching.

In his exposition of Exodus 3, Helmut Frey designates Moses as the first "apostle." In verse 10 of that chapter he sees the first commission for the archetypal apostle, Moses. God sent Moses to Pharaoh, saying: "Come, I will send

[5] *Ibid.,* p. 71.

you to Pharaoh that you may bring forth my people, the sons of Israel, out of Egypt." Frey comments:

> Every apostolate stems from the Lord, who is the highest authority, not only in heaven, but also in the realms of history. Basically, every apostolate has a double address, since the apostolate is a testimony of this highest authority in that area where these demands cross each other:
>
> (a) to the authorities and rulers who see the demands of the authority of God as a questioning of their own existence, and
>
> (b) to the congregation, which is totally unable, in itself, to understand its liberation.[6]

I believe this includes two essential aspects of the apostolic ministry. "I will send you to Pharaoh that you may bring forth my people . . . out of Egypt" — that is the dual commission of an apostle. He is the representative of the lordship of God in the world. Conflicts arise between the commissioned of God and those who believe that the power of the world belongs to them, because the lordship of God is not recognized in the world. On the other hand, the apostle represents the congregation of Christ in this world. He is to liberate them from their manifold ties with this world.

What kind of people does God send? To look at several of the names of apostles in the Bible, one might conclude that he chose particularly respected and powerful people. Moses had been trained in Pharaoh's court. Paul was a disciple of the famed Gamaliel and an emissary of the priests in Jerusalem. If, however, we consider the circumstances under which these two apostles were called, it immediately becomes clear that Moses was called after he had to flee from Pharaoh, after his own people had rejected

6 H. Frey, *Das Buch der Heimsuchung und des Auszugs* (1952), pp. 53f.

him, after he no longer received the recognition that had formerly been his; and Paul was sent out as an apostle at a time when he had lost every credit that he had ever had with his friends, after the priests persecuted him vehemently, and when he was unable to remain in Jerusalem any longer. Jesus did not send out the twelve when he was still the great prophet of Judea, but after his infamous death, after they had locked themselves in, in fear of the Jews, after they had been rejected by their own people and members of their own religion, and when no one would even so much as accept a slice of bread from their hand. I believe these facts are important.

To be sure, the personal call to apostleship occurred much earlier, when these men still enjoyed the respect of their fellow men. But the actual sending out followed only after everything that would, under normal circumstances, have given authority and access to the people, had been shattered, so that the authority no longer rested on human power and human influence, but in the power of God. Paul, Moses, the twelve, and many others were then able to act only in the power of God. Their human authority had been destroyed. Paul himself writes that God has chosen that which seems foolish in the eyes of the world, that which is despised, yes, that which is nothing anymore. That is the very thing God has chosen in order that he might destroy that which is something. And he declares that he considers everything as refuse compared to the high calling of Christ. The authority and power of the apostle is of a purely spiritual nature. An apostle has no chance whatever to achieve anything with the devices of this world.

That kind of apostolic ministry led to serious difficulties, particularly in Corinth. The Corinthians wanted an imposing leader figure like the heathen philosophers or the

Judaic "superlative apostles" (II Cor. 11:5). They wanted a strong apostle, not a weakling. But "God has placed this great treasure of the gospel into a weak vessel, which is the apostle, in order to show quite clearly that the power that exudes from the gospel originates in God, not in man (II Cor. 4:7). The human weakness is, in fact, a prerequisite for the workings of God."[7]

(b) *The prophets.* The New Testament mentions persons to whom the gift of prophecy has been entrusted and also those who have the ministry of a prophet. Acts 13:1 indicates that there were both prophets and teachers in the congregation at Antioch. The grammatical structure of the sentence in the original Greek seems to denote that Luke is distinguishing here between three prophets (Barnabas, Symeon, and Lucius) and two teachers (Manaen and Paul).[8] In addition, Acts mentions as prophets Agabus (Acts 11:28; 21:10), Jude, and Silas (Acts 15:32). According to I Corinthians 14:29 prophets played a role in the worship service of the church.

Although many Christians have received the "charismatic" gift of prophecy, in some Christians this charisma is so profound as to enable the congregation to recognize that God has entrusted the ministry of a prophet to one or another of its members.

What constitutes the commission of such men? Of Jude and Silas we are told that they "comforted and strengthened" the congregation. This apparently refers to a general, congregation-building encouragement. However, not every minister who somehow lends encouragement is necessarily a prophet.

Irenaeus designates the prophets as "those to whom God

[7] Gerhard Friedrich, *Amt und Lebensführung* (1963), pp. 18f.
[8] W. M. Ramsay, *St. Paul the Traveller and Roman Citizen* (1895), p. 65.

sends His grace from above . . . and then they speak where and when God pleases" (*Against Heretics*, I, 13, 4). Calvin writes in the *Institutes*: "Paul gives the appellation of 'prophets,' not to all interpreters of the divine will, but only to those who were honored with some special revelation" (IV, 3, 4).

Those who are able to discern the so-called secrets of the heart, of which I Corinthians 14:24f. speak, constitute a special case of this prophecy. Apparently, persons had arisen in the congregation who had been imbued with the particular gift of revealing the secrets of the heart, a charisma that the New Testament also attributes to Jesus (John 2:25; 6:64; 13:11; Mark 2:8) and to Peter (Acts 5:3f.). In the early church we encounter it, for example, in Ignatius. The letter of Ignatius to the Philadelphians was written to a situation in which sectarians had broken into the congregation. They had declared to Ignatius that they were true believers, and when he arrived they acted as if they were Christians and would give full allegiance to the church. As soon as he was absent once more, they resumed their destructive influence. Ignatius writes: "For though some would have deceived me according to the flesh, yet my spirit is not deceived; for I have received it from God" (VII, 1). Even if Ignatius had not recognized, as a man, that this kind of person was active here, the Spirit clearly convinced him, so that he was able to see distinctly who was not living as a true Christian.

In the Eastern Church this charisma is especially prominent in the so-called staretz. Thus, for example, the Russian Orthodox Archimandrit Serafim writes:

> A staretz is a person who has totally dedicated himself to God, and who receives the grace from him to read both the present, past, and future in a human soul. God lives in him and acts through him. Most of them are monks, but

one also meets them as laymen of both sexes. God bestows this gift upon whom he will. The staretz, like Jesus, has an intimate relationship with every soul. He frequently receives hundreds of callers in one day, who come to him with their questions, worries, sorrows, and problems. And God works through him. The staretz is able to show everyone what God's intentions are for him, and specifically for him.

He works in gentle, even tender love, he comforts and consoles, but rarely commands. His humble and Spirit-filled words change the person completely, to a total transformation.[9]

Such prophet figures have occasionally arisen in Western Christendom as well, for example, Nicolaus von Flüe and Vianney, the priest of Ars. Walter Nigg writes about the latter:

Vianney possessed the gift of being able to understand the soul of a man in an instant, and without any lengthy explanations, to feel at once what spiritual trouble was afflicting it. How well did he understand the wayward, pusillanimous heart of man! With a very few words he knew how to bring comfort to the sorely tempted soul, he swiftly and decisively answered the most complicated questions of conscience, and gave counsels which invariably revealed a complete understanding of the situation in question. The priest of Ars penetrated right into the emotions and feelings of his spiritual children and could read their souls as though in a book. He had a clear-sighted vision which often enabled him to foretell to a man what would happen to him in the future.[10]

A second kind of prophecy is that reported of Agabus in Acts 11 and 21. This consists in foretelling how the con-

[9] Archimandrit Serafim, *Verklärte Schöpfung* (1959), p. 11.
[10] Walter Nigg, *Great Saints* (1948), p. 249.

crete events of the present will affect the immediate future, in order to induce the church to act in a certain way. Thus, for example, Agabus foretells a time of starvation, in Acts 11, in order to induce the congregation to initiate supportive ministries. Eduard Schweizer writes: "The Lord, the Kyrios himself, speaks through the prophet and thereby gives very explicit instructions."[11] We are reminded here as well of Jesus' prophecy about the destruction of Jerusalem. In Luke 21:20ff. Jesus described exactly how this destruction would come about. The Christian church in Jerusalem took Jesus' prophecy seriously, and emigrated to Pella when the Romans approached. Thus they survived the catastrophe. It is remarkable to read the gruesome reports in Josephus' *Jewish War* of the destruction of Jerusalem in the year 70, and then to realize that no Christians were destroyed in this city because they had listened to the prophecy of Jesus and left. Eusebius notes that it was only "when those that believed in Christ had come thither from Jerusalem, then, as if the royal city were entirely destitute of holy men, the judgment of God at length overtook . . . and totally destroyed that generation of impious men" (*Church History*, III, 5, 3).

Finally, there is a third type of prophecy. In the great prophetic book of the New Testament, the Revelation to John, it is reported that the prophet John saw events of the distant future, not in the concrete way that events of the near future were related, but rather as an insight into the great relationships of world events and a perspective on history. Thus prophecy not only supplies facts about the very near future, but the service of the prophets also provides an effective basis to help the congregation master its situation in this world, in that it is given hope.

[11] E. Schweizer, *Der Gottesdienst im Neuen Testament* (1958), p. 11.

Prophecy may be clearly distinguished from prognosis and apocalyptic. Prognosis is foretelling on the basis of known laws of nature. I can, as it were, foretell a sun eclipse or when a certain star will turn cold. But prognosis is not concerned with the realm of history. Wherever human intervention is possible, I can only very questionably make a prognosis. Prophecy deals with the realm of history.

Apocalyptic, on the other hand, covers up the actual prophecy. It presumes to show precisely when and where and how things will happen; it designs charts of salvation; it draws cards for the future, from which it will deduce when the rapture will take place and how many years later the millennium will commence. This type of apocalyptic was widespread in late Judaism. For example, apocalyptic constructed an exact Messianic expectancy on the basis of Old Testament prophetic utterances. According to these apocalyptics, it was not only known where the Messiah was to be born, but also how he would appear and how he must reign. The appearance of Jesus did not coincide with what the apocalyptic had prophesied. Thus, this false apocalyptic bears part of the blame of Jesus' crucifixion. It may be that many of today's apocalyptics, too, will be terrified, in the light of eternity, at what they have done with genuine biblical prophecies, how they have twisted them by means of apocalyptic into the exact opposite of what they were.

In contrast to apocalyptic and prognosis, prophecy is an irritating form of revelation. It maintains the whole anger of the gospel. History remains indecipherable, but it is no longer confused. We receive no handy formula according to which we can work, but we are given so much cause for trust that we need not resign. Prophecy reveals the future, but it shows no details. Prognosis makes us restless: I must act myself, for if I wish to escape from the predicted calamity, I have to do something. Apocalyptic cradles us in false security and makes us proud: nothing can happen to us for, after all, we know everything as it will be. Prophecy, on the other hand, grants us the peace of God on one side, for we know that no one will be able to tear us from the hand of God. On the other side, it arouses a high sense of responsibility since we know that God never acts automatically, that he is neither restricted to an evolution nor to a plan of salvation, but that God only does what he does in history as his church follows him. A prophecy will not fulfil itself "automatically," but only fulfils itself through men who act accordingly. The prophecy of doom Jonah predicted for Nineveh was not fulfilled because the Ninevites reacted enough to the appeal of God contained in that prophecy of doom to fulfil the actual will of God. The actual intention of the prophecy of doom becomes evident, then, for even the prophecy of doom is a call to salvation!

(c) *Evangelists.* Philip is designated as an evangelist in the New Testament (Acts 21:8). (We know from Acts 6:5 that Philip was also a deacon at that time.) Timothy is encouraged to do the work of an evangelist (II Tim. 4:5). What is an evangelist?

The most distinct description of the ministry of an evangelist is found in Acts 8:5-7:

> Philip went down to a city of Samaria, and proclaimed to them the Christ. And the multitude with one accord gave heed to what was said by Philip, when they heard him and saw the signs which he did. For unclean spirits came out of many who were possessed, crying with a loud voice; and many who were paralyzed or lame were healed. So there was much joy in that city.

Later in the same chapter we read: "But Philip was found

at Azotus, and passing on he preached the gospel to all the towns" (vs. 40).

This description makes it clear that the evangelists were not residents of one area, but that their commissions took them beyond their own place of residence. Furthermore, we learn that they proclaimed the gospel in full authority and that the proclamation of the gospel was apparently related to the gift of healing and driving out of demons.

Rene Paché defines it this way: "Evangelists are people who are filled with love and power, capable of winning people for Christ, both within the religious milieu and outside of it."[12] Therefore they are concerned with a mission to the people and to the world in its broadest sense.

In post-apostolic times the evangelists were virtually designated to be followers of the apostles. The early church historian Eusebius writes:

> And there were many others besides . . . who were known in those days [the second century], and who occupied first place among the successors of the apostles. And they also, being illustrious disciples of such great men, built up the foundations of the churches which had been laid by the apostles in every place, and preached the gospel more and more widely, and scattered the saving seeds of the kingdom of heaven far and near throughout the whole world. . . . Then starting out on long journeys they performed the office of evangelists, being filled with the desire to preach Christ to those who had not yet heard the word of faith (*Church History*, III, 37, 1-2).

Heinrich Rendtorff states:

> Evangelization is the preaching of conversion, directed to the masses, by the individual charismatically gifted evangelist. The distinctive features that raise their preach-

[12] Rene Paché, *La plenitude de Dieu* (1946), p. 56.

ing above that of the customary sermon are fearlessness in the choice of methods, spiritual decisiveness in carrying out the proclamation, the passionate involvement of the evangelist himself, the intensive prayer, colloquial popular language, the personal spiritual ministry.[13]

According to Rendtorff, then, there is a "customary" sermon and a sermon that goes beyond customary proclamation, which he calls evangelization. Already in ancient times a distinction was made between the language of worship, which was held in a measured, formal language, and the so-called Cynic-Stoic diatribe, which was characterized by colloquialism, "fearlessness in the choice of methods," "passionate involvement" of the speaker, and the like. What Rendtorff says about the evangelists could— as far as formal matters are concerned — also be said of the Cynics and Stoics, who traveled about and "evangelized" for their philosophy.

But in the final analysis the issue of evangelization is not method. "Fearlessness in the choice of methods" is not an end in itself. The sole reason for an evangelist to use anecdotes, jazz, films, or colloquial idiom is to induce people to listen, to arouse them out of their lethargy, to speak with them in a common language that they are able to understand. In the final analysis, though, the evangelist is concerned that God's Spirit meet the spirit of man!

There is in every man a "God-shaped blank," a longing for God. Man seeks something that he does not know himself. He searches for fulfilment in life, peace with God. The Spirit of God, which speaks through the evangelist, will only speak into this blank or emptiness, and thereby kindle a hope in the people who listen to the evangelist, a hope that can finally be realized as faith. Only where God

[13] H. Rendtorff, "Evangelisation," in *Die Religion in Geschichte und Gegenwart* (3rd ed.).

himself — where God's Spirit itself — is present in the evangelist will this Spirit be able to touch the human spirit as well in such a way as to foster new life. No method or rhetoric — it matters not how profound — is able to awaken new life in man. Only the Spirit of God is able to do that. And so it is absolutely essential that the evangelist not speak in his own power, that he not emphasize his evangelistic methods, but that he be at the disposal of the Holy Spirit.

This is clear in the example of Jonathan Edwards, one of the great American revivalists of the eighteenth century. Edwards wrote down every word of his sermons before delivering them. Nearsighted, he would stand in the pulpit with the sermon in one hand and a candle in the other. Yet not only were people converted by his preaching, but it moved some of them to fall to the ground in the face of their sins — all as a result of the impact of the Holy Spirit.

(d) *Shepherds.* Shepherds are spiritual counselors. While the evangelist presses forward and conquers, the shepherd preserves and keeps. The most beautiful description of the ministry of a shepherd is that found in Psalm 23. Jesus himself is the shepherd of his church, according to John 10:12; I Peter 2:25; and Hebrews 13:20. According to John 21:15ff. Peter received a share in the shepherding ministry of Jesus.

Since Paul enumerates the shepherd ministry in the lists of ministries of the whole church, apparently the shepherd ministry was not only prevalent in the local congregation, but in the church at large as well. One might wonder why this was necessary, if each congregation had its own "shepherd" or "pastor." But if we look at the situation as it is today we can only conclude that this gift of spiritual ministry is not adequately practiced in every individual congregation, so that we could not do without the shepherd responsible for the church as a whole. I am personally acquainted with people who have traveled hundreds of miles in order to speak with a person who has the authority of a spiritual counseling ministry.

The shepherd-ministry aims at the upbuilding of man's personality. The shepherd is not concerned only with hearing confessions — others can do that also — but with finding an insight into the life situation of the individual. The shepherd does not give advice based on strict rules and laws, but rather he strives to accept each person as an image of God, to intuit and feel, in conversation with the person, just what *that* person sitting before him *now* needs *in his situation.* (A different person, in the same situation, may need something altogether different!)

This concerns the actualization of love to this person in question; it concerns the full realization of man's humanity in this individual! God has given a special charisma and a special functional ministry for this purpose, and this must be at the disposal of the whole church.

Gerhard Tersteegen, for example, was such a shepherd of the "whole church." Ranking him with the "greatest spiritual ministers of all time," Walter Nigg writes:

> His cure of souls, born of that compassion of God's which allows its sun to shine over good and evil, took the form of a great gentleness which could never bring itself to condemn a man, but which brought a genial understanding to his spiritual needs. We shall not have penetrated, however, to the innermost essence of this if we explain it only by Tersteegen's fine psychological feeling which he derived from his study of the mystics. Naturally the cure of souls in his case . . . included an intuitive knowledge of psychology. But Tersteegen's central endeavor was always to place man in God's radiance, to lead him out of his spiritual despondency into the Divine

light, "through the narrow into the immeasurably wide." This man of stillness was a human who knew all about the ultimate, darkly divined longing of the soul for the supernatural meaning of human existence, but at the same time he was well aware of the only way whereby such a longing might be fulfilled.[14]

Nigg quotes a remark of Terstecgen to the effect that anyone who deals with souls must be like a nurse who leads a child on a leash only to shield it against danger and falling, but otherwise lets the child have free play.

(e) *Teachers.* In addition to the ministry of the prophets in the congregation at Antioch, there was also the ministry of the teacher. These men added to the charisma of knowledge the gift of teaching. For the ministry of teaching it is not enough to have knowledge; one must also be able to transmit it to others. A specific charisma, the gift of teaching, is essential for transmitting the subject matter. The church father Chrysostom describes the difference between a prophet and a teacher in the following words: "In the prophet, all pronouncements are brought forth by the Holy Spirit; the teacher on the other hand sometimes teaches on the basis of his own understanding." Thus it is apparent that human thinking is included in the transmission of a teaching, whereas this is not necessarily so in every instance of prophecy. It is possible that the prophet is so steeped in God as not to listen to his own speech at all. By contrast, the teacher's mind is constantly engaged.

It seems to me that God's Spirit is stirring up the teacher's intellect in order that he bring forth teachings that have been directed by the Holy Spirit. This clearly shows that the danger exists in teaching for the intellect (man always has this tendency) to make itself independent and draw conclusions, on the basis of personal involvement,

[14] Walter Nigg, *op. cit.,* pp. 217-18.

that are no longer guided by the Spirit. It is a danger particularly strong where one adopts criteria from the realm of science or philosophy and applies them to the spiritual realm. It is impossible to transfer logical or scientific rules without further ado to the spiritual realm. The fact that this occurs again and again has led to some of the most disastrous false teachings recorded in church history.

The teacher is in constant danger of making false assertions if he is not in constant contact with the Holy Spirit. Because this is such a great danger, the New Testament warns against making dogmatic statements too hastily. Most of the schisms in Christendom have originated in false doctrinal opinions. Those who expound their own opinion, without assignment from God, create inestimable harm. (Verse 14 of our text speaks of this kind of false teaching.) Paul even perceived this danger within himself, and so he was extraordinarily critical of himself. He knew that he had made certain pronouncements in direct dependence on the Holy Spirit, but, fearing for a time when he may succumb to the temptation of revoking these pronouncements, he writes, "even if we or an angel from heaven should preach to you a gospel contrary to that which we preached to you, let him be accursed" (Gal. 1:8). God expects that his teachers will perform their ministry faithfully (Rom. 12:7); and the teachers will one day have to give account of their ministry (II Tim. 4:2).

There is a fine testimony from the fifteenth century of how knowledge is bestowed upon a charismatic teacher. A fellow-monk reported the following about Johannes Ruysbroek:

> He loved, when the spirit came upon him, to plunge into the loneliest recesses of the beautiful forest surrounding the monastery. There, on a tablet of wax, he noted

down the suggestions of his mind, and afterwards, at home, extended the draught. Sometimes, for want of grace, there would be an interruption to his writing for whole weeks. On resuming it, however, he at once recovered the thread; as, we are told, used also to be the case with Plotinus, another man of contemplation. In this manner, under the suggestion of the Holy Spirit, as he himself believed, and as was indicated by the name of *ecstatic teacher* which he received, originated his numerous writings. . . . [15]

The charismatic teacher is concerned with teaching the old message in a new situation in such a way as to preserve the old message. Moreover, the teacher must transmit the "word of knowledge" in a way the congregation is able to understand.

To amplify what is meant by "word of knowledge," let us look at an example of how this is concretely possible. In the milieu of the Old Testament, sun, moon, and stars were considered to be gods or godlike powers and were worshipped by man, who felt dependent upon them. The old message that God is Lord over his creation is clarified in Genesis 1:14-19 with this background in mind in such a way that it becomes evident that sun, moon, and stars are depicted as lamps *created* by God to *serve* mankind. The world thus became deprived of its divine attributes. But in this very act God's lordship was clearly brought to the fore and man received the opportunity of dominating the world, on assignment from God. (When water is no longer a divine force of chaos, but two parts hydrogen united with one part oxygen, one can confidently examine it under the microscope. Consequently modern science owes its origin to this loss of divine attributes in the world. Thus

[15] Quoted by C. Ullmann, *Reformers Before the Reformation* (1855), II, 34.

the heathen Babylonian world-picture is demythologized and the lordship of God over all creation is distinctly proclaimed. It is true, of course, that when man exercises his prerogative to rule independently of him who gave him this assignment, nature again becomes a threatening chaotic power — cf. Gen. 6:5ff.)

How then do we understand the expression "God is Lord" in the New Testament? In the Hellenistic world it was no longer customarily believed that the stars were identical with deities. But demonic powers — intermediate beings between heaven and earth — were seen in connection with them (Eph. 1:20ff.). The Gnostics believed that these intermediate bodies were not subordinate to the lordship of God, but had their own inherent laws.

Again, the old message that God is Lord is retold in a new situation in such a way that the message remains unchanged. It is now presented in the statement that God is Lord over all the powers; that these are not lords in their own right, side by side with God, but that they are incorporated into the *pleroma;* that everything listed in Ephesians 1:21 belongs to the attributes of God.

Therefore, the assignment of the charismatic teacher today still consists of telling contemporary man that Jesus is Lord over all the powers that seem to threaten him, and that everything that endures and happens in this world cannot endure and happen without Christ.

Origen, one of the greatest teachers of early Christendom, prefaced one of his interpretations of Scripture with these words:

> We plead for riches, out of the fulness of the Son of God, in whose total fulness God was pleased to dwell, for the ability to tell it powerfully, to receive a superabundance of thoughts that are in no way empty ones, so that the gospel may be revealed to us in a measure equal to

our seeking. In doing so we would not omit anything that needs to be investigated and, along with explanatory writings, to be believed; at the same time, we should not like to be unduly detailed, nor to misconstrue the meaning of Jesus our Savior.

Would that God might send us the Logos himself, who reveals himself, in order that we, through the gift of the Father, might contemplate his depths (preface to *Commentary on John*, Book XX).

## 2. *The Function of the Ministries for the Whole Church*

(*a*) *The immediate goal*. The function of the ministries for the whole church is first of all equipping the saints (vs. 12). The word translated as "equipping" is a medical technical term (*katartismos*) in Greek, which denotes setting bones back into their proper place. Beyond that this expression has the basic meaning of "replacing something back to its correct position." In that sense this word is used in Mark 1:19f., where the disciples are "repairing their nets" — putting them back in order again.

A sound boxing of the cheek will sometimes succeed in resetting a dislocated jawbone. But the work of one concerned with the ministry of the church as a whole is more frequently like that of net mending. This ministry is a laborious task. Cautious mending, which the "shepherds" in particular must accomplish, is of utmost importance in order that the saints may be equipped or set right once more. We can understand Paul's summary of his ardent wish for the congregation (II Cor. 13:9): "What we pray for is your improvement [your being put back into your rightful place]." Only rightly set members are able to perform their assignment satisfactorily.

If anyone wishes to exercise his charisma privately, outside of the functional relationship with the body of Christ,

71

he creates harm. Everything that a Christian does in relationship with the body of Christ helps his neighbor. Everything that he does independent of the body of Christ, and therefore independent of Christ himself, does not help his neighbor in the final analysis (cf. John 15:5). Furthermore, Christ has initiated the offices of the whole church "for the work of ministry." This describes unequivocally the function of a servant. He has no particular power or position of nobility, only a particular work, a "ministry," that realizes itself in service. With this he does not, basically, differentiate himself from other members of the congregation whose charismatic gift also realizes itself as "service" (I Cor. 12:5). His only distinction is that he has received his commission from Christ to perform a special function continuously.

Finally, Christ instituted the ministries "for the building up of the body of Christ." In mixed metaphor (literally: for the "house building" of the body of Christ) Paul is here comparing the congregation with a house to be built. God himself is the master-builder (I Cor. 3:9 — "for you are God's building"). Paul is the "architect" (literally so, according to I Cor. 3:10). He has laid the foundation in Corinth. Others (these would be the bricklayers) have continued to build on this foundation. The possibility exists, according to I Corinthians 3:12, that these bricklayers may continue to build with either good or bad building material ("gold, silver, precious stones, wood, hay, stubble"). But the poor building material does not withstand the test (I Cor. 3:15 — "his work is burned up"). Therefore it does not serve to build up with bad materials. A good minister is one who builds well.

(b) *The long-range goal.* How long will the ministries for the whole church be essential? Paul's answer is *"until*

*we all attain to the unity of faith.*" The long-range goal of
the ministries is thus unity of faith.

Paul includes himself in this sentence; he has not attained this goal either and in fact is unable to achieve this
as a single individual. The unity of the faith can only be
realized in the totality of the body. All Christian living is
action in faith. Every use of the charismata is action in
faith. Faith stands at the beginning of the Christian life
(Heb. 11:6; Eph. 2:8). It grows as a fruit of the Holy
Spirit (Gal. 5:22); that faith which can move mountains
is a gift of the Holy Spirit (I Cor. 12:9; I Cor. 13:2). The
Christian life is "through faith for faith" (Rom. 1:17).
Faith grows in proportion to our practice of it. The more
we entrust ourselves to God, the more our confidence in
him will grow, because we constantly experience that God
does not forsake those who trust him. Unity of faith means
that we are all united in a sincere and unshakable confidence in the one God.

There are still (potential) members of the body of Christ
who have not yet accepted the faith. Furthermore, there
are other members of the body of Christ whose faith is
weak, who must be strengthened time and again in the
face of their doubts and temptations. Apostles, prophets,
evangelists, shepherds, and teachers are essential for leading the members of the body to a unity of faith. And this
must go on until "the one herd and the one shepherd" have
become a reality. Ecumenicity is the unity of all believers
on the inhabited earth. This does not refer as much to a
unity of confession of faith or liturgy on the part of the
various members of the body of Christ, as to a united
confidence in God.

Also, the members of the body of Christ are to be led
*"to a knowledge of the Son of God."* Faith always precedes
knowledge; and knowledge follows immediately after faith.

Knowledge can only be gained through love. In Hebrew usage the words "to know" and "to have sexual intercourse" were synonymous (see, for example, Matt. 1:25). The implication is that knowledge is always acquired in the most intimate community of life with God, that is, in faith and love. The highest goal in the world, for Paul, is "to know Christ"; he considers all else in the world to be as refuse in comparison to this (Phil. 3:8).

Many churches today do not even begin to display such a desire for the knowledge of Christ. Many things are considered more important than the knowledge of Christ. Knowledge grows exactly the way faith does — through experience with Christ. Knowledge of Christ does not grow through our activity, but through prayer — quiet resting before God — through unselfish submission to God. This is conveyed in a song by Gerhard Tersteegen:

> *Thou the light that fillest*
> *All the endless heavens,*
> > *Shinest on my face,*
> *As the tender flowers*
> *Joyfully unfolding*
> > *In their silent grace,*
> *Whilst the sun beholds them —*
> *Thus my soul is still,*
> *Thine the glorious power,*
> *Thine the mighty will.*[16]

Anyone who allows Jesus to work in him in this manner will come to know him much better than someone who merely listens to lectures about Jesus and reads books about him.

Schisms will no longer be possible within Christendom once a unity of faith and of "knowledge of the Son" is

[16] Transl. Frances Bevan, in *Hymns of Tersteegen* (1894), p. 47.

realized. The body of Christ will have attained *"to mature manhood, to the measure of the stature of the fulness of Christ."*

The mature Christian stands in contrast to the child (vs. 14; cf. I Cor. 3:1; 2:6; Heb. 5:13, 14). The body of Christ can only be fully mature when the individual members are fully mature. Naturally, the individual member only grows to the limits of his possibilities — just as in the physical body the hand does not generally grow as long as the foot nor the eye as the ear. Growth does not proceed indefinitely, but there is a certain full-grown maturity of the body of Christ. The body is able to achieve its fulness or *pleroma.* The body of Christ is fully mature when everything that pertains to it has been assimilated and processed by it. This is only possible if love grows in us and Christ penetrates us more and more. Then the individual becomes Christ to his neighbor, and the congregation in its totality represents Christ in this world. When Christ has penetrated his body to the last fiber, the body of Christ is full-grown and mature.

Since the body of Christ is not yet full-grown, the ministries for the whole church are still essential today, for they were designated for that time "until we all attain to the unity of the faith and to the knowledge of the Son of God, to mature manhood, to the measure of the stature of the fulness of Christ." The ministries for the whole church will be necessary as long as the church is still "growing up" into him who is the head, into Christ (vs. 15).

The claim that these ministries for the whole church are still essential today is not an undisputed one. Let us examine this question a bit more closely before proceeding to our next topic.

The question that is particularly disputed today is whether it is still possible to have apostles. Many commentators opine that the apostolate was a one-time, unrepeatable ministry of early Christendom.

Of the early church leaders whose writings are classified as "Apostolic Fathers," only the document called the *Didache* talks about the ministry of living apostles. Even there, the difference between them and the prophets is not clear. According to the *Didache* there are no false apostles, but only false "prophets" who assumed the ministry of the apostle themselves (cf. II Cor. 11:13, which speaks of false apostles). Ignatius and Polycarp already viewed the apostles as men of the past, and Eusebius, in his *Church History*, designated the evangelists as followers of the apostles.

Four different views are advanced by contemporary theologians. First there are those who consider the apostolic ministry as a one-time arrangement. Eduard Schweizer, for example, believes that the apostles held a nonrepeatable, special position. He writes: "One may speak of disciples of the apostles, but not of followers in their ministry."[17]

A second view is that the apostolic ministry has been discontinued due to the fault of the church. This opinion has been defended by Heinrich Thiersch, who argues that the apostolic ministry ceased because the congregations were not ripe for it. In consequence of this, the charismata ceased as well.

A third position is that the apostolic ministry is only necessary in particular situations. Thus John Calvin, discussing Ephesians 4:11, writes: "Of these [the five ministries named], only the last two sustain an ordinary office in the Church: the others were such as the Lord raised up at the commencement of his kingdom, and such as he still raises up on particular occasions, when required by the necessity of the times" (*Institutes*, IV, 3, 4).

[17] E. Schweizer, *Gemeinde und Gemeindeordnung,* 24b.

Finally, some theologians argue that the apostolic ministry is a constant ministry in the church. Watchman Nee differentiates between the apostle of God (Jesus), the apostles of Jesus (the twelve), and the apostles of the Spirit (Paul and all other apostles). He claims that a cessation of the Spirit-apostolate was not intended at any time. Ralf Luther writes in a similar vein:

> Christ did not have only twelve apostles. The New Testament shows us apostles in all congregations (Eph. 4:11; I Cor. 12:28), men who have been empowered to keep alive the relationships between Christ and the congregations, and also to establish these in new areas.
>
> The apostolate in the New Testament is not an extraordinary arrangement that was essential at a particular time, but an orderly service that is always essential (although the twelve apostles have a peculiar significance all their own).
>
> As soon as we no longer have apostles, i.e., authorized emissaries, the connections will be severed between heaven and earth.[18]

In fact, the New Testament nowhere suggests that the apostolic ministry was intended only for first-generation Christians. On the contrary, we constantly encounter people in church history whom we designate as apostles.

To the question as to whether we may still have *prophets* today, Paul Tillich answers:

> The prophetic spirit has not disappeared from the earth. Decades before the world wars, men judged the European civilization and prophesied its end in speech and print. There are among us people like these. They are like the refined instruments which register the shaking of the earth on far-removed sections of its surface. These people

[18] Ralf Luther, *Neutestamentliche Wörterbuch* (7th ed.), pp. 11f.

register the shaking of their civilization, its self-destructive trends, and its disintegration and fall, decades before the final catastrophe occurs. They have an invisible and almost infallible sensorium in their souls; and they have an irresistible urge to pronounce what they have registered, perhaps against their own wills.[19]

God still sends his prophets today, with the commission to verbalize that which is hidden, in the individual, in the Christian community, and in the world at large. When that is done, all false appearances are destroyed and all self-confidence is shaken in its very foundations:

> Most human beings, of course, are not able to stand the message of the shaking of the foundations. They reject and attack the prophetic minds, not because they really disagree with them, but because they sense the truth of their words and cannot receive it.[20]

What is true of apostles and prophets is also true of the other ministries in the church as a whole. The ministry of evangelist, which, according to Calvin, is one of the ministries the Lord awakened "in the beginning of his Kingdom," is today generally recognized in the churches again. It is to be hoped that the ministries of the "prophets" and "apostles" may find a similar recognition.

As long as the church is in the stages of growth, ministries for the church as a whole will be necessary. Rudolf Bohren clarifies growth within the church using the following images:

*The building.* "The church in the New Testament, the church as manifestation in this world, is not a completed building, but a becoming and growing one. . . . A house in

[19] Paul Tillich, *The Shaking of the Foundations* (1948), pp. 7-8.
[20] *Ibid.*, p. 8.

the process of construction is unsupported and weak."[21]

*The bridge.* "The wedding will only take place in the future. . . . As long as the bride is still on the way, the apostle will still have to vie for the purity of the maiden . . . . What happened to the old Eve is not to be repeated in the case of the new Eve."[22]

*The body of Christ.* "The body of Christ is not yet full-grown! It must be goaded to further growth. Discipline is necessary in order that the growth not be retarded by harmful influences."[23]

God has ordained these five ministries we have been talking about so that the building may be completed, the bride may remain unmolested, and the body of Christ may grow. The church has despised the ministries of Christ. That is why the building is not yet completed; the bride has entered into a relationship with the world — she has not remained untouched; and the body of Christ is still in the infant stage. God is yet willing to start anew with us, to give us gifts and ministries in order to complete his church. Will we accept God's offer this time?

Which special functions are brought into play in the various ministries, so that the church may achieve its goal?

*The apostle* safeguards the relationships as a whole, the connections between the individual congregations, one to another. In doing so he must endure disruption. He risks being ground up between the individual groups and circles. An apostle will never endorse only one form of congregation. He will always keep the total body in view. An apostle can never be a sectarian or confessionist.

*The prophet* is a necessary complement to the apostle.

[21] R. Bohren, *Das Problem der Kirchenzucht im Neuen Testament* (1952), p. 36.
[22] *Ibid.,* p. 40.
[23] *Ibid.,* p. 46.

79

He accompanies the apostle step by step, assuring him of God's will in each particular situation. He strengthens the congregation through the word of Jesus (Acts 5:22). He warns against dangers and taking the wrong way. Time and again he draws the attention of the congregation to the overall aim and shows it the next step.

*The evangelist* completes the body of Christ by winning the missing members. He hastens to those areas, wherever the Spirit drives him, where there are people whom God wishes to save, who also belong to the body, but who are not yet members of it.

*The shepherd* secures the individual members of the body of Christ in their personal walk of faith, by a spiritual ministry of follow-up.

*The teacher* initiates people into the proper knowledge of the faith and into a right understanding of Scripture. He offers meaningful insights into God's word and will. In this way he makes use of the point-of-view of the apostles and prophets to the greatest extent, so that they might understand and retain all the members of the congregation.

Though the ministries for the whole church are as significant as ever for the Christian church, it becomes more and more questionable whether they can still be performed by individual persons. Many problems today can best be dealt with and solved by teams. Perhaps this is why the representatives of the ministries for the whole church today are not primarily individuals, but ecumenical groups and brotherhoods with an *apostolic* or *prophetic* task; missionary societies and boards with an *evangelistic* task; retreat houses that perform all sorts of *pastoral* or shepherd ministries; and seminaries and other institutions of learning in which Christian *teaching* is carried on. There are definitely individuals within these groups in whom "group-charisma" is prominent, but these individuals must be supplemented by the other members of the group. The complex problems of today's world cannot be conquered by lone individuals anymore.

Rene Paché, in his commentary on Ephesians, writes:

> How is it that our churches have become so poor and, as a rule, have only the one ministry remaining, that of the pastor? Surely this is the main reason: that the "preparation of the saints" and "the building of the body of Christ" have progressed to such a small degree. One member has, in fact, replaced all the other members (it is of little consequence whether this happened intentionally or whether it was forced into this position). The result of this development is a serious disruption of balance and in a deadly atrophy of the remaining members who have been robbed of their function. Let us pray that, in our visible church, the essential services, that is, the function of essential members, not be suppressed any further, and let us act accordingly! Christ, the head, has given these functions to his body long ago. Let us not hinder them anymore, so that they will be able to manifest themselves!

## 3. Dangers of Growth

(a) *Lack of independence.* One of the main dangers in the growth of the body of Christ is the lack of independence of the members who are "tossed to and fro and carried about with every wind of doctrine" (vs. 14a). The immature members of the congregation are totally dependent on their environment and their own frame of mind (cf. James 1:6; Heb. 13:9; Jude 12, 14). The immature one falls prey to every doctrinal snare. The congregation addressed in the letter to the Ephesians, for example, had fallen into the teaching of the Gnostics. Such immature members have no power of discrimination. They always endorse that which they heard most recently. Paul calls this kind of Christian a spiritual child.

It is the responsibility of the teacher above all to lead the members of the congregation to clear conviction and firm opinions, not, however, to a barren system of doctrines. The teacher will strive instead to lay a good biblical foundation that will enable independent growth.

(*b*) *Seduction.* Seduction comes about "by the cunning of men, by their craftiness in deceitful wiles" (vs. 14b).

False teachers play games with Scripture and people alike. Truth is of no consequence to them. They do not care about their neighbor, but only about their own advantage. Often this is done with conscious deceit, presented with glowing arguments imbedded in magnificent logical conclusions and statements of contemporary philosophy. The Greek word used for deceitfulness here designates the conscious malice behind which, finally, is Satan (in an old manuscript the word "devil" has been inserted into this verse; cf. Eph. 6:10ff.).

The ministries for the church as a whole are absolutely essential in order to lead the congregation out of its dependent attitude and guard it against false teachings.

## 4. Healthy Growth

"Speaking the truth in love, we are to grow up in every way into him who is the head, into Christ" (vs. 15).

If the child is not to remain a child, he must grow. How does this growth come about? It happens through love and truth together. Truth without love is brutality. Love without truth is sentimentality.

Truth is the transparency of a person who has nothing left to hide from God. Confession is vital for attaining such transparency. There must be nothing in my life that I am not prepared to tell to at least one person. Only thus can I really learn to know myself, and only thus can I meet my neighbor "in truth." Only after I have pulled the beam from my own eye, do I gain the privilege of alerting my brother to the sliver that is in his. Love belongs to truth, however. Truth can only affect the heart of a man when it is imbedded in love. Paul describes the practical manner in which love works in I Corinthians 13.

In what direction does the growth of a believer proceed? Into the body of Christ, that is, into Christ. And the body is able to show healthy growth only when all the members are in their rightful place, when all the members perform their special functions, when all the members are under control of Christ the head, that is, when they have a constant and vital relationship with Jesus. This is not brought about by activity, but by resting in Jesus. Then Jesus will draw us to himself, as we read in II Corinthians 3:18: "and we all, beholding the glory of the Lord, are being changed into his likeness from one degree of glory to another."

What are the practical implications of this? Let us use a comparison to answer this. Ancient sailors, unacquainted with the compass, steered towards the pole star. They knew that they would never be able to "reach" this star, but they held straight to their course by heading towards it. There are countless false teachings in the world today, which try to steer us away from our course and to lead us astray. They buoy us up with false promises of a happy life, independent of God, but the end of this is sin and misery.

Jesus is the true light. To grow into his likeness means to hold him before our eyes continuously, to strive to emulate his example. We know, to be sure, that we will never "reach" him (at least here on earth), but in looking at him (as ancient sailors looked at the pole star) we are able to hold to our course. Our life is guided by the right goal as long as we look at him. This is not only true of the individual Christian, but of Christian groups and denominations as well. The more unequivocally our gaze rests on Jesus, the closer we are to one another. "Christ, from whom the whole body, joined and knit together by every joint with which it is supplied, when each part is working properly, makes bodily growth and upbuilds itself in love."

Everything that happens in the body of Christ has its origin in Jesus. He himself, as the elevated head, passes through the members of the congregation and submerges the cosmos into the *pleroma,* thereby building up the congregation as well as himself. The ministries for the whole church, which are rooted in love, have a guiding function in this growth and in the upbuilding of the church. They recognize the necessary flexibility of the body of Christ and look after the interrelationship of the members. The ministers for the whole church work with an enormous commitment. Building up the body of Christ is not a cheap affair, especially today after centuries of dissension have worked against it. But no one is ever overcharged in upbuilding the body of Christ. The ministry is always in proportion to "the measure of faith which God has assigned him." In Romans 12:3 Paul stresses that no one must exceed the measure allotted to him by God. God does not expect more of any man than he has endowed him with, nor does he expect less. To put it succinctly in the words of an old adage: Anyone who is active beyond his measure becomes nervous; anyone who does less than God requires of him becomes discouraged. Origen, the Greek church father, wrote:

> When Jesus acknowledges something, he does not do so merely in respect to the size of the contribution. He gives greater acknowledgment to those who do a menial task with all the power at their disposal, than to those who ac-

complish a greater feat with less competence than lies in their power (*Commentary on John*, XIX, 8).

Christ himself moulds the members of his body together. He himself is the internal order of his body. Just as in him all the charismata are united, so he is also the prototype of all church ministries. In his person he is apostle, prophet, evangelist, shepherd, and teacher. But he is also bishop, presbyter, and deacon. Charismata and ministries are functions of the one Christ. Christ is the only acting one, in everyone and through everyone. Just as the charismata are reflections of the functions of the body of Christ, so the ministries are reflections of Christ as head. Inasmuch as a minister is present in a congregation, so Christ is present there. People are to read the being of Christ in the being of the minister. (That is why the New Testament tolerates no compromises in the life-style of its ministers.) The practical result of Christ's headship is seen in his love, his sacrificing himself for the church, and his work of sanctification of the church (Eph. 5:25ff.). Similarly, the minister legitimizes his position in that he loves the congregation, sacrifices himself for it, and becomes deeply involved in the sanctification of its members.

Christ orders everything through love. Love is the principle that permeates everything and which creates order. As the gifts of grace are empty without love (I Cor. 13), so too the ministries are empty without love. But since no man has an innate capacity to love as Christ loves, the minister must ever again recede so as to enable Christ to work through him. The important aspect is not that people who need Christ meet a person, but that they meet Jesus himself, the arch-apostle and archdeacon.

# 6

## *Gifts and Ministries*

As they heard these things, he proceeded to tell a parable, because he was near to Jerusalem, and because they supposed that the kingdom of God was to appear immediately. He said therefore, "A nobleman went into a far country to receive kingly power and then return. Calling ten of his servants, he gave them ten pounds, and said to them, 'Trade with these till I come.' But his citizens hated him and sent an embassy after him, saying, 'We do not want this man to reign over us.' When he returned, having received the kingly power, he commanded these servants, to whom he had given the money, to be called to him, that he might know what they had gained by trading. The first came before him, saying, 'Lord, your pound has made ten pounds more.' And he said to him, 'Well done, good servant! Because you have been faithful in a very little, you shall have authority over ten cities.' And the second came, saying, 'Lord, your pound has made five pounds.' And he said to him, 'And you are to be over five cities.' Then another came, saying, 'Lord, here is your pound, which I kept laid away in a napkin; for I was afraid of you, because you are a severe man; you take up what you did not lay down, and reap what you did not sow.' He said to him, 'I will condemn you out of your own mouth, you wicked servant! You knew that I was a severe man, taking up what I did not lay down and reaping what I did not sow? Why then did you not put my money into the bank, and at my coming I should have collected it with interest?' And he said to those who stood by, 'Take the pound from him, and give it to him who has the ten pounds.' (And they said to him, 'Lord, he has ten pounds!') 'I tell you, that to every one who has will more be given; but from him who has not, even what he has will be taken away. But as for these enemies of mine, who did not want me to reign over them, bring them here and slay them before me'" (Luke 19: 11-27).

Jesus is on his last journey to Jerusalem, where he will participate in the Passover. Multitudes of people are accompanying him. As he nears Jericho, the last large town before Jerusalem, the expectation of these multitudes rises to a climax. At the entrance to Jericho Jesus heals a blind man (18:35-43) and proclaims the good news of redemption to Zacchaeus, the chief tax collector (19:1-10). Jesus' total work of redemption is summarized in these last two activities before his entry into Jerusalem. One is reminded of Jesus' first appearance, recorded in Luke 4:16ff., at which he quoted a passage from Isaiah and applied it to himself: "The Spirit of the Lord is upon me, because he has anointed me to preach good news to the poor. He has sent me to proclaim release to the captives and recovering of sight to the blind. . . ." Jesus was saying no less than that the Kingdom of God had begun with his person. The whole time of his public ministry was essentially nothing other than an interpretation of this biblical text. And so we can understand why the expectation of the throngs rose to its highest pitch just before Jesus' entry into Jerusalem. "They supposed that the Kingdom of God was to appear immediately."

Jesus corrects this expectation in telling the parable of the gifts. According to Luke's account, this parable was told in direct relationship with the conversion of Zacchaeus — evidently in Jericho.[1] We can well imagine Jesus, sitting on the flat roof of the tax collector's villa with Zacchaeus and his friends and looking across to the winter residence of King Herod, which his son Archelaus had finished magnificently. Perhaps Jesus was thinking of that son of Herod while telling this parable, which was, in so many respects, reminiscent of Archelaus. King Herod, erroneously called "the Great," had not only ordered the children of Bethlehem to be killed ( Matt. 2:16), but many of his own sons as well. He continuously altered his last will and testament — even on his deathbed. His last testament stated that the country was to be divided among his sons Archelaus, Philip, and Antipas. Archelaus was to be king, and the other two were to officiate as his coregents. Since Palestine belonged to the Roman Empire, Archelaus was forced to obtain substantiation of his kingship from Caesar Augustus in Rome first. He went to Rome for this purpose. But Archelaus was very unpopular because of his cruelty. Fifty reputable citizens of Palestine followed this pretender so they might beg Augustus not to give him the kingdom, for they did not wish that this man should rule over them. Augustus, nonetheless, confirmed Archelaus as monarch, although the title of "king" was not to be granted to him until a certain probationary period had elapsed. After his return Archelaus took cruel revenge on his enemies, ordering that several thousand of his fellow citizens who were hostile to him be massacred, while he rewarded his friends.[2]

These historical events form the basis and outer frame of the parable. They had occurred in the not too distant

[1] A. Plummer, *A Critical and Exegetical Commentary on the Gospel according to St. Luke* (1960), p. 438.
[2] Accounts of Herod and his sons may be found in Josephus' *Jewish Wars*, Book II, and *Jewish Antiquities*, Book XVII.

past, and consequently many citizens of Jericho could well remember Archelaus, though he had since been deposed by the Romans and replaced by a Roman procurator. Naturally, not all the details of the parable coincide with those of the historical facts. History merely constituted the framework for the message Jesus wished to impart to his people. His basic concern was to clarify to his listeners that the Kingdom of God "will not appear immediately," but rather that — as in the case of Archelaus — a definite time-span had to elapse before Jesus would take final possession.

### 1. Rebels and Slaves

During the interim between the time Jesus goes to his Father and the final fulfilment of the Kingdom of God, there will be two groups of people: "enemies of Christ" and "slaves of Christ."

The sign of the "enemies of Christ" consists of an inscription they have, consciously or unconsciously, placed on their banner. It reads: *"We do not want this man to reign over us."* Those who represent this view are not, according to the text of the parable, distant heathens who do not even know Jesus by name. They are his fellow citizens. Certainly, at that time this referred to the Jews first of all. To us today this saying points out clearly that one may outwardly be numbered among fellow citizens of Christ without actually submitting himself to his sovereign claim. Church history proves that the decisive opposition against Jesus frequently does not stem from the ranks of the "evil world," but from the apparently pious. Already in the New Testament there is reference to people who hold the form of religion but deny the power of it (II Tim. 3:5).

Frequently the real enemies of the gospel are not heathens or atheists; rather, they are those who know about

Jesus, but who refuse to bow to his sovereign claim. When Jesus declared that he was sending his disciples out "as sheep into the midst of wolves" (Matt. 10:16), he meant by wolves first and foremost those who were related to him by birth and religious affiliation. Friedrich Heiler, commenting on this text, says: "Church history teaches us that the wolves are not to be found solely among enemies of the church, but sometimes also among church leaders, and that whoever takes Christ's mission and task seriously will have to fight with them just as with the declared enemies of religion and church."[3]

Christian church history offers an abundance of substantiations for this statement. The real enemies of the gospel are frequently those for whom Christianity merely constitutes one sector of life, the center of which is their personal ego, who are not prepared to permit another to have dominion over them. Such people have always been ready to cry "Lord, Lord" and to take an active part in worship — but they have not been ready to change their lives and to do the will of Jesus. Bearing the semblance of a godly life, they lack its power. Jesus imparts no power for the execution of personal desires and representations. Power is only available to the Christian in order that he may place his life into the hands of Jesus and permit the Holy Spirit to be active through him. Jesus does not grant power that is independent of himself. He either bestows himself, or else he bestows nothing at all. Jesus himself is the power.

What happens to those who — by word or by way of life — announce, "We do not want this man to reign over us"? Jesus' parable supplies the answer to this: "But as for these enemies of mine, who did not want me to reign over them, bring them here and slay them before me" (vs. 27).

[3] F. Heiler, *Ecclesia Caritatis* (1964), p. 318.

This is a gruesome verse, one that hardly seems to fit into the New Testament. Therefore, let us examine it under a microscope, as it were, and establish some basic considerations relevant to the problem of punishment for the sinner.

What does this verse really say? It says, simply, the end of autocracy is destruction. We are reminded of Jesus' saying: "Whoever would save his life will lose it" (Mark 8:35). Anyone who believes he will find greater happiness in not permitting God to reign over him will — like the prodigal son in Luke 15 — experience that the other side of such a life of profligacy entails hunger and degradation. The abundant life (John 10:10) is only possible in following Jesus. No ultimate fulfilment of life, no true happiness is possible independent of Jesus. Whoever loses his life for Jesus' sake will save it (Mark 8:35). This is not merely a reference to consolation in some distant beyond; it includes an abundance of life's fulfilment on earth (Luke 18:28-30). Whoever does not believe in Jesus — that is, submit his life to him — will remain in a condition of death and judgment.

John says it this way: "Whoever believes in the Son has eternal life; but whoever remains disobedient to the Son will not see life, but the wrath of God remains upon him." Friz Hochwaelder concludes his drama "The Public Prosecutor" with the sentence: "One can do just as one pleases in this world — but one must pay for it." If one wishes to live independently of God, he must bear the consequences of his actions. God's judgment consists of the fact that he does not force us to observe his ordinances of salvation, but that he respects our freedom to such an extent as not to intervene when we destroy ourselves (cf. Rom. 1:18ff.). Whoever does not wish to have Jesus reign over him as King is employed in his own self-destruction. God created

91

no hell, and he punishes no man, but we prepare hell for ourselves.

Sadhu Sundar Singh describes the following vision:

> Once, a man who had led a wicked life came to the world of spirits in my presence. When the angels and saints tried to help him he suddenly began to curse and revile them, saying: "God is totally unjust. He has prepared heaven for such fawning, slavish minds as you are, and he throws the rest of mankind into hell. And yet you call him Love."
>
> The angels replied: "Certainly, God is love. He has created mankind in order that man should live in eternal bliss with him, but mankind in its obstinacy and by the misuse of his free will, has turned away from him and has prepared its own hell. God never throws any man into hell, nor will he do that, but the sin-ensnared man creates his own hell. God never created any hell."
>
> At the same time one could hear the extraordinarily beautiful voice of one of the angels above, which said: "God permits that this person be taken to heaven." The man quickly stepped forward, accompanied by two angels; however, when he reached the door of heaven and saw that sacred, light-pervaded place and its transfigured blessed inhabitants, he felt uneasy. "Just look," the angels said to him, "What a beautiful world that is! Walk on, see our beloved Lord, who is sitting over there on his throne!" He looked through the door, but when the Sun of Righteousness revealed to him the impurity of his sin-stained life, he recoiled in violent revulsion on account of himself and fled so precipitously that he did not even make a halt at the intermediate stage, the world of spirits, but flew through them like a rock, and plunged headlong into the bottomless abyss.[4]

[4] Sadhu Sundar Singh, *Gesichte aus der jenseitigen Welt* (1962), pp. 41ff.

In another vision Sadhu heard the voice of an angel declaring:

> "Look, it is not at all necessary to pronounce judgment. The life of a sinner proves itself guilty. It is not necessary to tell him so, nor to bring witness against him. The punishment of a sinner begins in his heart while he is still in the world; but here he feels its full results. God has decreed that goats and sheep, i.e., sinners and just ones, separate from each other according to the essence of their being. God has created man for life in the light, where his spiritual well-being and joy endure for ever. That is why no man can possibly be happy in the darkness of hell; but neither, as a result of his sin-spoiled life, can he feel at ease in the light. For that reason a sinner will always find himself in hell, no matter where he turns. Compare the position of the just one to this. How exactly opposite it is in kind; released from sin, he is in heaven everywhere."[5]

No matter what one thinks of the visions of Sadhu Sundar Singh, one thing is clear: they very forcefully express the New Testament idea that the man who pays no attention to God's ordinances, who does not desire that Jesus reign over him, destroys himself. God has given us the freedom of determining and adjusting our lives according to our own inclinations. Each new act of decision stamps our ongoing life and makes the following (positive or negative) decision easier. One becomes practiced in sin, just as one does in the dependence upon Christ. I have met many people who have said, after confessing a severe guilt, "It is totally inconceivable to me that I could have gone that far." But it was not really inconceivable at all, for in each case the "large" sin had been preceded by practice in "little" sins, most of which had not been taken seriously

[5] *Ibid.*, p. 46.

since the destructive consequences were not immediately evident.

The word in the parable which we have translated as "slaying" means literally "to open the jugular vein." In ancient Greek texts this term is used exclusively to speak of the butchering of animals. In the Greek translation of the Old Testament it is the technical term for the cultic slaughter. "To open the jugular vein" means that death does not occur instantaneously, but that life ebbs away slowly, as the blood flows from the body. So the life of one who wishes to live independently of God flows away from him; he is "slaughtered" before the eyes of God.

Although this parable concludes with such a somber point of view, we know from the total message of the New Testament that Jesus is prepared, at any instant, to intervene in this self-destructive process of man. He is ready to give new life to everyone who recognizes his mistake and subordinates himself to Christ's reign. But on the other hand the New Testament does not conceal the fact that there will, one day, be a "too late." "When once the householder has risen up and shut the door, you will begin to stand outside and to knock at the door, saying, 'Lord, open to us.' He will answer you, 'I do not know where you came from. . . , depart from me, all you workers of iniquity!'" (Luke 13:25, 27).

The second group of people in this parable is designated as "slaves of Christ." What is the meaning of this expression? Adolf Deissmann tells, in his *Light from the Ancient East*, of an old ceremony in which a fictitious purchase of a slave was made by a god. The former lord would come to the temple with his slave, sell him there to the god, and receive the purchase price from the temple treasury, where it had been deposited beforehand by the slave or a patron. The slave became, thereby, the property of the god, although not his temple-slave, but rather one who was protected by the god. He was entirely free in relation to man, particularly in relation to his former lord. An official document was displayed concerning the act of liberation. Hundreds of such documents of slave-liberation are chiseled into the stone of the wall of the Apollo temple in Delphi. The text of such a document reads something like this: "The god Apollo is buying one slave X from mister N to freedom, at the price of five pounds of silver. . . . " Frequently it was expressly mentioned in these liberation documents that re-enslavement of the freed person was punishable by a severe penalty

In the New Testament we find many allusions — some of them word-for-word — to such slave-liberating documents. Paul, above all, described Christians as people who have been purchased from the slavery to sin (Titus 3:3), death (Rom. 8:20f.), the law (Gal. 4:1ff.), people (I Cor. 7:23), anti-godly powers (Gal. 4:8f.) by Christ, for a "purchase-price" (I Cor. 6:20; 7:23). They are now slaves of Christ (Rom. 6:16; I Cor. 7:22; Eph. 6:6; Rev. 22:3 and others) and may not again be made slaves either of man or of any other power.

To be a slave of Christ means to be independent of everything that would induce us to be inconsistent with the will of Jesus. It does not mean, however, to be under a forced lordship to Christ. We have been freed to our essential humanity, to our real function, by Christ. He has installed us as stewards (Luke 12:42). He expects us to carry out this service conscientiously. That has been the subject of these pages.

## 2. Equivalent Gifts

According to verse 13 each slave received one pound from his master. Apparently this refers to an amount of silver worth approximately one hundred dollars. The actual amount of money is irrelevant in the parable; it appears that the only point to be noted is that all the gifts are of equal value. (That distinguishes this parable from one told by Matthew.) The total sum that the ten slaves receive amounts to ten pounds. The number ten is the number of perfection in the Bible, from which we may conclude that in any case only the entire local congregation receives the totality of the gifts. It is in this sense that Paul writes to the congregation at Corinth, "You are not lacking in any spiritual gift" (I Cor. 1:7). Certainly, every member of the local congregation has *his* God-ordained function, but all the functions are of equal value. Thus there is no cause for pride nor for feelings of inferiority. Everyone receives the one Holy Spirit, individualized and concretized according to personal appropriateness for each receiver.

When the master commands his slaves to "trade with this till I come," the thought is expressed that the practice of the gifts of grace is related to the return of Christ, that is, it has to do with the essence of the service rendered between Jesus' ascension and the final fulfilment of the Kingdom of Christ. The form of the Greek verb for "come" that is used here does not express a one-time event; it indicates a continuous process. One might, therefore, translate this as "during the time in which I am returning."[6]

What actually constitutes the return of Christ? It consists in the establishment of his Kingdom on this earth. How does this come about? Jesus says, "The Kingdom of God is not coming with signs to be observed; nor will they say, 'Lo, here it is!' or 'There!' for behold, the Kingdom of

[6] F. Godet comments on this verse: "The entire time of Jesus' absence is a continuous coming again." *Commentar zu dem Evangelium des Lukas* (1872), p. 387.

God is in the midst of you" [or: "internally within you"] (Luke 17:20f.). When Jesus states that the Kingdom does not come with signs to be observed — conspicuous phenomena — he means literally, "not in such a way that an uninvolved bystander would be able to observe it." Wherever Jesus was active, destroyed creation was made whole again. When Jesus spoke this word to the Pharisees, he could say to them that the Kingdom of God was *in the midst of you*," in his person. Today Jesus lives in believers. So, the words "the Kingdom is internally within you" refer to us. Destroyed creation is again being made whole in Christ's work through Christians. To the extent that we allow Christ to work through us, we are instrumental in building the Kingdom of God. Our contribution is not enormous, to be sure (the slaves receive only a rather meager pittance); nonetheless, it adds to the transformation of the world and initiates a process that concludes in the final fulfilment of the Kingdom of God. Christ does not return in a way that one could observe as an uninvolved bystander; his return occurs in that we permit ourselves to be drawn into the transforming process.

There is a false and a true waiting for the future. I should like to clarify this through an example. For hundreds of years Israel knew of the Old Testament promises that the nation would one day return to Palestine and that the land which had become a desert would bloom again like a rose. For hundreds of years pious Jews all over the world have hoped for the fulfilment of these promises. They imagined that at the coming of the Messiah everything would be changed with one stroke, so that even an uninvolved bystander could observe it. Some Jews have recently begun to reflect on this in a different way. They have said, "If it is true that God has given this land of Palestine a promise, if a Jewish state is actually to arise there, if the land is to become fruitful once more, then we do have a promise, if we move into this land against all resistance, construct irrigation systems and reforest the bare hills." These Jews undertook what seemed humanly hopeless and, step by step, their experience was that God did not forsake them. I do not wish to say by this that the State of Israel is already a part of the Kingdom. I only want to clarify that there are two ways of taking the promises of the Bible seriously. One way is to lay one's hands in his lap and wait until something happens; the other is to take seriously the word of Jesus in our parable: *"Trade with these till I come."*

God places the spread of his Kingdom in our hands. He has an enormous trust in us. If we do nothing, nothing will happen. On the other hand, when we permit Jesus to work through us, the old world is broken down, piece by piece, and the Kingdom of God is built up. Similarly, when a caterpillar turns into a butterfly, it does not do so without a stage of transition. The live caterpillar does not simply change into a butterfly; it becomes a pupa first of all. In the pupa the bodily frame of the caterpillar is broken down, piece by piece, and the butterfly is constructed. When the butterfly one day emerges from the pupa he does not in any way resemble the caterpillar any longer, but he would never have become a butterfly if the necessary process of transformation had been missing in the pupa. When the Kingdom of God is fulfilled one day, it too will be totally different from our present world. And yet the Kingdom of God will not be fulfilled without the process of transformation that Christ is already bringing about on this earth through Christians today. It is certain that this process (exactly like that of the pupa) will come about in concealment.

Still, there should be visible evidence of "progress" here

and there. What appearance might such a progress have? Let us look at the development of Christianity. Surely, there is a great deal in this realm that looks more like regress than progress. The cry we hear in many ecclesiastical quarters, "Back to the early church!" is understandable. Even so, it seems to me that it is also possible to view church history positively. I believe that nothing of that which bore the germ of developmental possibility in the original church has been lost. Indeed, I believe the opposite — much of what was still undeveloped at that time has matured during the course of church history. Certainly, one may be annoyed at the great number of denominations within Christendom, but many an essential element and constituent of faith, which was part of early Christendom, could only be preserved in this manner.

Count Zinzendorf wrote in December 1747 that "in every established denomination in Christendom lies a specific thought of God, which can be maintained by no other denomination. Every Christian denomination has a treasure which it must preserve, according to God's command, to which it alone has the key, so to speak. The house of God cannot be built by one denomination alone, one must combine them."

To be sure, the emergence of the butterfly includes the fact that believers in various denominations must find and confront each other anew, in order then to recognize, with amazement, the fulness of the Kingdom of the *one* church of Jesus Christ.

The people to whom our parable was told supposed that the Kingdom of God would "appear (visibly) immediately." The word that Luke here uses for "immediately" has the sense of "without extensive preparation." Jesus wards off this wrong concept by clarifying, in the parable, that his "return" will be well prepared for.

But the other fact must also be considered. Despite all the preparations, something totally new will appear at the conclusion of the "return" of Christ. Then it will become evident that Christ is actually physically present on this earth, and that he reigns. It is certain that his body will then not — as once his lowly body was — be limited to one geographic location, but will encompass the whole world and create healing on the entire earth. The New Testament even indicates that his "body" will have cosmic dimensions.

### 3. Varied Results

Although the slaves are requested to achieve something, that is, to work, to do something, Jesus still makes it clear that it is not the slaves who are actually the workers, but the gift itself. Look at the words of the parable: *"Your pound* has made ten pounds more" (vs. 16); *"Your pound* has made five pounds" (vs. 18). It is not the slaves who multiply the gift; the gift multiplies itself when it is used in the right way.

I think Jesus meant to say by this that *God himself* is at work. It is not our own activity that counts, but the fact that God himself is active through us. The more we retreat and allow God to work through us, the more God's gift will be able to accomplish something through us. The more we ourselves are active, the less God will be able to perform something through us. Detached from Jesus, our activity is "nothing" (John 15:5). When Paul states (I Cor. 15:10) that he has worked more than anyone else, he imbeds this remark, at the beginning and end, in the statement that it is not he, but God who has worked through him (likewise he says in Gal. 2:20 that "it is no longer I who live, but Christ who lives in me"). As God worked through Christ then, so Christ works today through the members of his body. Not what we do for Christ is important, but what we permit him to do through us. When we are requested, as "slaves," to accomplish something, our activity consists only of remaining in a right dependence upon God, so that he may be able to work through us.

When the parable discusses three different results, this does not have to do with the fruits of human activism, but with degrees of dependence on Jesus. Let us look at these three outcomes separately.

The third slave represents those who have feelings of inferiority, who think themselves short-changed in respect to gifts. This type of person despises his gift. He is evidently of the opinion that he could be a good slave to his Lord, even without special gifts. No doubt that sounds very humble, yet it is really quite selfish. People with feelings of inferiority are often "proud" people, not content with what was given to them because they believe they deserve something better. They are people who constantly pursue side-goals — perhaps with great exertion — and imitate models whom they admire. They imagine that they are accomplishing something great for God, and that God is pleased with them indeed. They despise the gift with which God could do something through them, perhaps because they suspect, unconsciously, that they would attain less human fame and honor with the management of this gift than with their Christian activism. Perhaps they even pride themselves, in a feigned humility, thinking "I have no special gifts," and do not notice that they are lying to God and the world. Instead of giving themselves to the community, they burden their fellow Christians with a superfluous facsimile of someone else. Whoever does not give himself to his neighbor, in his originality, gives nothing, but hides his actual gift in a napkin. A facsimile of someone else contributes nothing to the building of the Kingdom of God.

The designation of God as "severe" (vs. 21) is typical for Christians who have such proud feelings of inferiority. Their image of God is a false one; their God is very small, "harsh, sour, unfriendly" (so one should translate this verse literally). Perhaps they had a mean or unjust father who became the source of their God-image. Perhaps that is why they have the idea of a "God" who lies in ambush, waiting to catch them at something bad, so he may thoroughly rap their fingers. Such people constantly run about with feelings of guilt. Conscience-stricken over the most laughable trivialities, they enact at the same time, untroubled by their so-called conscience, the grossest deeds of unkindness (Matt. 23:24).

Anyone who believes that God is "severe" has a false God. The New Testament says that "God is love" (I John 4:16). Paul tells us what love is and how it acts in I Corinthians 13. Love never demands more than it gives. Love does not expect perfection from imperfect beings, but it educates them. The total life of the Christian is growth. That is why God loves imperfect people. To grow means nothing other than to let oneself be loved by God, for God's love transforms. If someone wants to exert himself in bringing about his own perfection, he does not need God's love and consequently he does not experience it either. God remains "severe" for him. It is in fact quite difficult for one to work with his own powers and ignore the gift by which God would be able to work through him.

What happens to the unfaithful slave? The gift is taken away from him. Whoever despises his God-given charisma loses it. God does not work through him who will not let him do so.

Is the slave then lost eternally? Our text says nothing of

that. I think the statement in I Corinthians 3:13-15 applies to him: "Each man's work will become manifest; for the Day will disclose it, because it will be revealed by fire, and the fire will test what sort of work each one has done. If the work which any man has built on the foundation survives, he will receive a reward. If any man's work is burned up, he will suffer loss, though he himself will be saved, but only as through fire." That which our own activism has accomplished will not withstand the fire. However, he who belongs to the slaves of Christ will escape with his life, even though only "as through fire." The fact that the unfaithful slave is not eternally condemned has (understandably!) angered the "severe" Christians of all times. It is therefore not astonishing that an old manuscript of our parable adds: "Throw the useless slave out into the utter darkness — where there is howling and chattering of teeth." Whoever has a severe God deals severely with his fellow-Christians as well. How tragic that such Christians are unaware that they speak their own judgment therewith.

What is the meaning of the question that the Master put to the slave: "Why did you not put my money into the bank, and at my coming I should have collected it with interest?" What do we imagine this bank to be? One interpreter of the last century comments that "the Lord will ask him who has not been working, 'Have you at least been praying?'" But how can we possibly say "*at least* praying"? What *more* can man do than pray — above all, if it is not an activistic prayer, but a God-given one? We must look, therefore, for another explanation.

First of all, if the slave had placed the money into the bank, it would not have been hidden. God wants his gift of grace always to express itself freely and openly. It will not permit itself to be hemmed in by dogmatic and moralistic systems, nor by principles and viewpoints. Too tight an organization can also prevent the working of the Holy Spirit. A Roman prefect once said to Basilius, a father of the early church:

> "Do you know, Basilius, you are an intelligent man, but I believe that the church is not too well organized, that brings numerous difficulties at this time. One must improve upon all that." Basilius answered to this: "When everything is too well organized one forgets to invite the Holy Spirit. We love peace and calm, to be sure, but also situations which make us aware that God and the Holy Spirit must necessarily become active in us, for it is essential at every moment that the Holy Spirit work in us."[7]

Gifts of grace are a realization of God's love and life. God's life and love know no barriers. Anyone who finds preconceived opinions and immovable principles of faith more important than the free working of the Spirit will keep his spiritual gift hidden "in a napkin" and not give God the chance to work through him.

Thus, to put one's money into the bank means, first of all, that it is not being hidden in a napkin. But it also means, secondly, to be uninvolved in the increase of the money. We must be careful not to try to interpret every last detail of a parable; but since the discussion already concerns a bank, this may express the idea that it is possible for a gift of grace to multiply itself without special involvement on the part of him who has the gift. It is certain that a man who brings his gift to the bank cannot be a legalistic Christian, but he is more likely to be an unconcerned, indolent one. Perhaps this is a Christian who just lives at ease, from day to day, one who does whatever gives him pleasure, who lacks a particular, ordered prayer

[7] Eugraph Kovalevski, "Die Charismen in der Geschichte der Orthodoxen Kirche," in *Kirche und Charisma* (1966), pp. 81f.

life, but who, nonetheless, realizes that he is dependent upon God. Perhaps he is like Jonah, undoubtedly knowing that God wishes to speak through him, but not particularly pleased with this, and finally obeying only very reluctantly. If God were not able to work also through this kind of comfortable Christian, the spread of the Kingdom would be in a bad state. I believe that these somewhat slovenly Christians are the banks of God, from which he may sometimes draw more than merely minimal interest. Heinrich Böll writes in his *Irish Diary*, regarding the gifts of time and of money:

> When God created time, he created enough of it. Both wastefulness and economy are operative in the use of time, and, paradoxically, the time-squanderers are also the thrifty ones, for they always have time when one claims their time; just as one can always approach money-squanderers for money, so the time-squanderers are the tills in which God hides his time and keeps it in reserve for the case when some is suddenly needed to replace that which one of the thrifty has spent in a wrong area.

The second slave symbolizes a group of Christians who may possibly be somewhat related to the "bank Christians." These are people who know the word of God and who are, in principle, prepared to let God work through them. Time and again, they make room for the activity of God, so that the Kingdom may be spread in manifold ways. On the other hand, however, there are other times in the lives of these Christians when their own desires become overpowering, when they cling to their own plans and act in their own interests. Oswald Chambers once wrote: "Some of us have the new name in spots only, like spiritual measles."[8] God is able to work through such people, but only now and again. They are at God's disposal —

[8] Oswald Chambers, *My Utmost for His Highest* (1936), p. 164.

but not always. They constantly cross out God's will by their own will. But sometimes they do permit God's will to cross out their own. Many serious Christians belong to the group that the second slave represents. They place their entrusted gifts into the service of God, but only permit them to be operative to a limited extent.

What happens to such a slave? He receives neither praise nor criticism. He receives responsibility to the degree in which he has put himself at the disposal of God. His acknowledgment for right execution of his commission consists of an assignment that entails a greater responsibility. Note that the Kingdom of God does not consist of sweet idleness; even after our time on earth we shall have the opportunity to work, in a much larger dimension than has been the case here. The magnitude of the commission will, however, depend on the faithfulness with which we administer the gifts entrusted to us.

The first slave is an image of Christians who are totally at the disposal of God, those who can say with Paul: "I live, but not any longer I, for Christ lives in me." These are people who in happy tranquility let God work through them. They have totally subordinated all their own desires and goals to the will of God. They have experienced the reality that God alone gives life and fulfilment, and they know that anything we take according to our own will affords less happiness and fulfilment than what God wants to work through us.

Certainly, such an awareness does not arise in these people overnight. It is the result of a long process of education in which God takes possession of their lives, piece by piece. One Christian of our time describes how God clearly impressed this process on him. Day by day for a whole week God spoke to him, clarifying to him what it means to submit one's life to the lordship of Christ. He writes:

The Holy Spirit performed no mere superficial surrender, but he laid his finger on every single realm of my personal life, and I had to decide very soberly. The proceedings continued day after day. There where my old man had lived, he moved in with me, as God; he made it clear to me that, from now on, that which was permitted for Everyman, was no longer permissible for me. The Lord let me know that he would rid my total being of all avarice and all lust after wealth and possessions. Then I was confronted with the fact that I would never have the right to build a house according to my own desires. Other things, too, were traded in, including my ambition, and, on the fifth day, I could see where I stood with my good reputation and my prestige. By Friday night every point had been touched and I now knew exactly what was being offered to me: it was the choice between temporal and eternal gain. The Spirit summarized it all for me, in the following words: I shall under no circumstance permit you, henceforth, to carefully nurture even one thought concerned with your personal ego. The life which I will begin in you, will exist one hundred percent for others. You will never again be able to spare yourself more than Jesus was able to do during his time on earth. Are you ready for that? I bowed and said: Lord, I am ready.[9]

For most people this educational process of God will not come about in a week, but during a whole lifetime.

Imagine that we are living in a house whose doors are tightly locked and whose windows are completely covered. Thus it is totally dark in the house, even though the outside is bathed in bright light. If we now open one window a little, light streams in at once, and the rooms attain a certain amount of brightness. Perhaps we will discover

[9] L. Christenson, "Der Dorn im Fleisch," in *Die Bedeutung der Gnadengaben für die Gemeinde Jesu Christi* (1964), p. 122.

that there is dirt and disorder in the room. We can now bring things in order. But if we open one window after another, we will gradually discover more and more dirt, and we will have the opportunity to clean it all up. Finally, if we open all windows, the whole house will be filled with light.

A similar process takes place in the spiritual life. If we only open one window towards God a little crack, God's Spirit will enter our life. He will show us what is not in order in our life, and if we permit him to work in us, he will create order. The more we permit the light of God to enter still locked areas of our life, however, the more we will give God the opportunity to cleanse these areas of filth. To be sure, this process will not be completed during this life on earth — but if we allow God to educate us in this manner (God forces no one!), we will experience the truth of Luke 18:28-30 and John 7:38. The one gift will become ten, that is, the greatest measure of fruit.

What does the Lord now have to say to this faithful slave? He praises him as a faithful servant. The goal of his life has been achieved. He has fulfilled the commission of God, that is, God was able to work through him exactly what he desired to do. That does not mean that this slave had been "sinless" — God does not need sinless people — but rather that he has been totally at God's disposal.

Our life is a battle, as long as we live (Gal. 5:17). But the faithful slave will be able to say with Paul at the end of his life:

> I have fought the good fight, I have finished the race, I have kept the faith. Henceforth there is laid up for me the crown of righteousness, which the Lord, the righteous judge, will award to me on that Day, and not only to me but also to all who have loved his appearing (II Tim. 4:7f.).

The faithful servant receives authority over ten cities. The greatest possible responsibility is entrusted to him. In addition to his ten pounds, he receives an additional pound, that is, he not only receives the full measure of gifts, but an overabundance of them. Whoever allows himself to be totally used of God not only assists in the building of the Kingdom of God, but he himself receives life and its fulness. All potentialities and gifts unfold in him, and that which he still needs is given to him.